Scenes From
an
Ordinary Life:
Getting Naked to Explore
a Writer's Process
and Possibilities

Other books by Lou Orfanella

Composite Sketches (available from Fine Tooth Press)
Permanent Records
Summer Rising, River Flowing
The Last Automat

Scenes From an Ordinary Life:

Getting Naked to Explore a Writer's Process and Possibilities

Lou Orfanella

Fine Tooth Press

© 2005 by Lou Orfanella. All rights reserved. Printed in the United States of America.

No part of this book may be reproduced, stored in a retrieval system, or transmitted by any means, electronic or otherwise, without written permission from the author except in the case of brief quotations embodied in critical articles and reviews. For information address Fine Tooth Press, PO Box 11512, Waterbury, CT 06703.

First edition published 2005.

ISBN: 0-9766652-5-5

Library of Congress Catalog Card Number: 2005923644

Design by JJ Sargent ©2005
Cover art by Ivana Masic © 2005
Cover Author Photo by Justin Matthew Orfanella © 2004

This book is printed on acid-free paper.

In Memory of Suzanne Truran
(1914-2004)
teacher, mentor, friend

Acknowledgements

Some of the material in this book originally appeared, often in somewhat different form, in the following publications to which I offer my gratitude for the support: *Autograph Times, Baby Boomer Collectibles, Collectors Journal, English Journal, The Gannett Suburban Newspapers, Inland, New York Teacher, The Nimham Times Magazine, The Putnam County Courier, Statement, The Taconic Newspapers, Teacher Magazine*, and *Writer's Guidelines & News*.

To my family and friends who have supported my books and my appearances I am both thankful and humbled. To have others enjoy something I have created adds so much to the pleasure derived from the process. Thanks to JJ Sargent for his devotion to the literary arts, to Joe Ferraro for his help with this manuscript, to Ivana Masic for once again providing awe inspiring cover art, to my colleagues and students at Western Connecticut State University and in the Valhalla, New York school district for helping provide creative and intellectual environments, and as always to Marie, Justin, and Marygrace.

Contents

Introduction

I had an elderly uncle, Al, who took great pride in introducing me to the staff members who cared for him at the Somers Manor Nursing Home where he spent the last year or so of his life as, "My nephew, he is a school teacher." I in turn always took great pride in being introduced that way. It was far better than being recognized as the "voice on the radio" during my days as a disc jockey and newscaster or having someone comment on a publication that had appeared in a magazine or newspaper.

While it is always validating to have something accepted for publication, I consider myself first and foremost a teacher. Every writer I have ever read has at some level become a teacher to me. When I was an undergraduate at Columbia University, if you were not pre-med, or at least pre-law, you might have well have introduced yourself as "pre-death" and how dare you take up a spot in an Ivy League class if your ultimate goal was not to climb to the top of one of the "elite" professions.

As I move through life and acquire new experiences in and out of the classroom I find that I have things to say. I find also that from time to time, people like what they hear. Putting some of these things down on paper has been a big step. Do I for example have as much to say as the voices that have inspired me: Kenneth Koch, Bob Greene, Anna Quindlen, Mike Lupica, Pete Hamill, and all the rest?

Growing older has helped me realize how much certain periods, people, and places in my life meant to me. I also realized how much of it was slipping away, perhaps for good. I realized that as a writer, or the one I had hoped to become, I could not only capture "now" but could also bring back a lot of "then." Had I known earlier how much I would value the past I would have done more to preserve it. As I found more successes as a poet, journalist, and essayist, I realized that the past was all still inside of me somewhere. The possibility of helping others to realize the same was appealing. As a teacher I have that chance.

There are shelves and shelves of books about writing, including textbook after textbook about grammar and usage. Many focus on the technical aspect, the how to publish aspect, the different genres. What about one for the person I was? Someone who wanted to be a writer but did not know what a writer did, thought about, went about his craft?

My goal with this book is to share some of what I have found to be helpful in my workshops and classes. There, I tend to be very relaxed as far as curriculum, letting things take whatever direction seems to work. We write together, share, and shape things. Some of our pieces reach final form while others do not. The same happened in the writing of this book. I started with some main themes and areas I wanted to visit. Some new, some based on pieces previously published. Some of my columns and articles seemed to exemplify what I was aiming for in various sections so are included. Other times I was reminded of things I had written but never done anything else with. Where these random musings seemed to fit, where they might have been things I would share in a workshop to make a point, they appear here in the same unfinished form I would have shared with my students in those settings. I have also included a brief writing prompt at the end of each section that I hope will be useful. Try them, change them, and see where they take you.

In my writing workshops a kinship of sorts develops. A trust in each other and an intimacy that is essential in any relationship tend to emerge. What I hope this book has become is a writing workshop that can be visited when you are looking for a jump start or just a friend with whom to write. It is part memoir, part inspiration, part instruction, part literary scrapbook. I hope it will leave you with the feeling that we have met, worked together and become part of each other. The title of the book? I thought about some of the metaphors I have used in writing instruction. Strip-mining and time travel were high on the list, but "getting naked" is the one that seemed the strongest, the one that seemed to best exemplify the idea that the best writing comes from developing an intimacy between reader and writer where there is nothing to hide. It also allows writers to become more comfortable with, and more connected to, the beauty and value of their own lives, no matter how ordinary they might think them to be. Get naked and explore the possibilities.

~

List five things you were taught about writing. Then, list five things you like about writing. Think about how your lists are similar and/or different.

Getting Naked

At the height of the rock and roll era when everyone's constant companion was a trusty transistor radio powered by a rectangular nine-volt battery, the gravelly voice of disc jockey Wolfman Jack blared out of tiny speakers and from dashboards around the country enticing his listeners to, "Get naked!" As we cruised through endless summer nights with the soundtrack of our youth drifting through the clear night air, what the howling, scowling Wolfman was really trying to do was break down the wall we all build around ourselves. Without relying on psychological theories or jargon, what he was doing was inviting us to shed our inhibitions and be real with one another.

For many years I dreamed of becoming a published writer. I dreamed of going into my favorite Barnes & Noble store's periodical section and purchasing a glossy magazine with my byline in it, then strolling to the poetry section to pick up my latest collection. I thought I was prepared. I had degrees from Columbia and Fordham. I had written radio news copy and public relations releases. I was a successful teacher of writing at the middle school, high school, and college levels. Still I was not a "working" freelance writer and was afraid that I never would be. My writing was forced, uninspired, and largely incomplete. Maybe I did not know anything worth writing about. Maybe I had lived a boring, uneventful life. Then I remembered Wolfman Jack's plea. It was time to get naked.

To become fully immersed in the writing process, you need to learn how to be naked. This is not easy. Today, in spite of living in a society where the public is bombarded with sexual imagery and where the media constantly pushes the envelope when it comes to graphic language and nudity, individuals are more modest than ever. Being naked means taking risks. I recall the high school senior, who, upon returning from a weekend visit to a college explained that she was no longer planning to apply there because the dormitories had showers without individual stalls. "I could never take a shower in front of a bunch of other people," she explained.

We all have things we would rather keep hidden. Those are the things that reveal the most about us, and the things that will lead to the strongest writing. As I embraced the process and began writing articles and poems about things I cared about and knew about, I began to find more success as a writer. Meanwhile, to my surprise, a second benefit emerged. Not only did my own writing career take shape, but I became a much better teacher of writing as I was at last intimate with the process. "Get naked!" became the guiding principle for my students. We laughed about it at first, but they took it seriously and more and more they bared themselves in their writing. They were getting excited and passionate about their work by taking the same journey through self-disclosure that I had.

One young lady who had blossomed into a very enthusiastic writer asked one day, "But how can I get naked if I am not excited about my topic?" Fair enough. We cannot always choose our topics, but we can get naked with any topic. We can learn about it and try not to be intimidated by it. Some of us are never comfortable getting naked, but we need to learn to do it. As one boy explained to his classmates more succinctly than I did, "Sometimes when you go to the doctor you have to drop your pants and take a shot in the rear end. You don't like it, but you learn to deal with it and you will get better because of it."

Beyond our physical bodies, which we clothe, we also hide our emotional inner selves. Shedding our inhibitions is difficult just as being naked, while natural, is often uncomfortable and embarrassing. Just as removing one's clothing is revealing, so too is putting one's thoughts down on paper. Any kind of self-disclosure is risky and uncomfortable, but is also necessary in any successful relationship, including that which exists between the writer and the reader. I constantly remind aspiring writers that the strongest writing comes from that which you would most like to keep private; that which is the hardest to put down on paper. Sharing what we know about and are passionate about, putting it down on paper for all to see, is risky too. To be a writer, to be intimate with the writing process, you need to step into that shower regardless of who else is there. You must allow yourself to be exposed for all to see. Smile, hold your head high, and bask in the unclothed glory of knowing you have the soul of a writer, exposed, vulnerable, and free of the inhibitions that keep us from fully discovering who we are and what we have to offer.

"You're So Vein"

For my entire life I had managed to maintain a very serviceable relationship with my blood. It stayed in my veins, arteries, and capillaries, and I did not have to look at it. All in all, I found it quite an agreeable arrangement.

Now in theory I had always felt that donating blood was a good thing to do. I also, with little or no guilt, was content to cruise through life never having done so. I happily rationalized this to myself by being a big advocate of organ donation. Hey, take what you want as long as I can't feel it when you do. I am not really sure where I developed this irrational fear, too embarrassing to even talk about. As a kid, I rappelled off cliffs, canoed through white water, and spelunked in stalagmite-filled caves. None of those activities ever seemed to call for a particular mental toughness. Just the thought, however of rolling up a sleeve to donate a pint of blood had always been enough to induce a lightheaded, clammy, weak feeling accompanied by images of big thick needles leading to even thicker tubes dangling from huge bottles of dark red blood.

When my son was three and needed surgery to remove his tonsils and adenoids, the operation was considered routine and rarely required any transfusing of blood. Still, you can never tell and as a precaution my wife wanted to donate some ahead of time. I had no problem with it, after all, she was a more than willing donor and shared his O+ blood type.

Unfortunately, for health reasons, she was unable to donate at the time. Since this was precautionary, not necessary, it was not a case of my jumping into the hero's role and offering a bulging vein to save the day. Rather, I hoped to find some way out of it.

The day prior to my donating appointment I needed to go to the hospital blood lab to be crossed matched, having never been blood typed before. If I was not type O, well, I gave it the old college try. I could not recall enough high school genetics to draw one of those little tables to figure out what my chances of being type O were.

The technician who drew my blood sample had a gentle touch and the ease with which he worked gave me a glimmer of courage for the next day had I turned out to be compatible, though it quickly dissipated. I contacted the lab the following morning to obtain the result, which naturally was O+.

When I arrived at the blood donor center that afternoon, I was informed that they would first conduct a mini physical and then if things checked out, the blood would be collected. I figured that gave me a few more chances to be rejected as a blood donor.

A finger stick and the whirring of a machine showed that my hemoglobin level was 16.1, well above the minimum of 12.5. Vital signs were my only remaining means of escaping a date with vampirism. After removing the cuff the nurse informed me that my blood pressure was 128 over 74. I had no idea what those numbers meant. She said they were very good. My pulse rate was timed at 84 beats per minute, falling safely in the acceptable range of 50-100. My final chance for a reprieve was temperature. Surely there had to be some stray bug floating around in my system that would elevate it just enough.

The reading was 37 degrees Celsius. They have every base covered – nobody can ever remember that conversion formula. Is it five ninths or nine fifths, and do you add or subtract the 32 to get to Fahrenheit? An acceptable reading it turned out.

Having accepted the fact that I had reached the point of no return, I followed the nurse to an adjoining room where a young girl of thirteen or fourteen was just finishing giving blood. Not old enough to be donating for the general public, she was perhaps preparing for upcoming surgery. A technician told her that she could replace the large wraparound bandage with a band-aid for her graduation ceremony that evening. I was not sure I would be able to walk out of the room, and here was this kid planning to walk across a stage.

I told the nurse that I would do much better with the whole procedure if she did not tell me what she was doing. "Most people are the opposite," she explained.

I closed my eyes and followed her instruction to count to five and then squeeze on the wrapped-up rubber bicycle grip I had been handed. I had expected collapsed veins and numerous jabs with a needle before the blood started flowing, but none of that happened.

I continued the rhythmic cadence in my mind and squeezed each time I got to five. Soon, I opened my eyes and looked around the room. I avoided eye contact with my arm but was still doing better than I had expected. It was over much more quickly than I had anticipated. They said to sit for a while and drink some juice. I followed those instructions but surprisingly felt that as soon as the apparatus was removed from my arm, I could have walked out like nothing had happened. I kept waiting to feel like passing out; for the floor to come rushing up but continued to feel perfectly fine.

During the pre-donation signing of forms the nurse said that I would receive a donor card in the mail and that it would indicate the date on which I would be eligible to donate again. Having discussed my apprehension at the time we both sort of laughed when she mentioned that bit of information. Since then, however, I have donated two gallons with no end in sight.

~

Write about at least one personal matter or embarrassing situation that you would rather keep hidden. Read it out loud to yourself, and then share it with three other people.

How John Boy Walton Changed My Life

It began in 1971 when I first saw *The Homecoming: A Christmas Story* with its lead character John Boy Walton. This is the film that brought writer Earl Hamner's alter ego and his Blue Ridge Mountain clan to television. I was fascinated and inspired by John Boy, played by Richard Thomas. He would sit in his solitary room and scribble his intimate thoughts and dreams in Big Chief tablets. How I longed to become a writer like John Boy and fill blank pages with secret thoughts and desires and keen observations of the world around me.

John Boy wrote of the beauty the mountains in his backyard and the sounds of whippoorwills outside his window. He told stories of colorful characters like Miss Mamie and Miss Emily Baldwin, the spinster sisters who made bootleg whiskey and called it Papa's Recipe. He wrote of the wise advice of Grandpa Zeb, the family patriarch, and of the iron will of Grandma Esther. I was teetering at the edge of puberty in the middle of white bread suburbia. What would my life ever give me to write about?

Determined, I gathered my nineteen cent Bic pens and wide ruled tablets. I set out to do what John Boy did, to record the events of my life to provide inspiration on my journey towards becoming a real writer. Each time I started, I found myself discouraged. Day after day, I jotted down short businesslike entries listing events: got up late, went to school, nothing new happened, watched *All in the Family* (funny episode), went to bed. There was nothing important to write about. I assumed I had to write every day about what I *did* and to have done something significant that was worthy of being put on paper.

Frustrated, I would start journaling and stop, eventually starting anew then ultimately stopping again. When *The Waltons* became a weekly series, I had more opportunities to observe John Boy and to think about the way he wrote in his journal. I realized that I was going about it in an entirely wrong way. He did not write about going to school or listening to Jack Benny on the radio. He also did not write about big important things. I wondered what was left. The very things I thought were not important enough to write about were the very ones that would ultimately help me become a writer. I was not supposed to chronicle my physical act of passing through the day, but rather I was to take notice of the beauty of the little things and thoughts that made up those days.

I began to focus on the little things that were important to me, just as John Boy wrote about life's little moments and ordinary people. I realized that the woods behind my house where we would build forts and climb trees were every bit as majestic as the Blue Ridge Mountains. My grandfather's stories of working in the coal mines of Pennsylvania when he was a child were as colorful as Grandpa Walton's stories of his family's pioneer roots. Joe Greene, the square dance caller who ran the local paper store, was every inch the character the Baldwin sisters were. Years later when I became a published writer, I learned to incorporate all of those preserved memories into my poems and articles.

My own philosophy as a writer and as a teacher of writing was taking root as I watched John Boy fill his journals. I learned that appreciating the beauty of ordinary things is important. I learned that every experience we have is significant and worth holding on to. Writing helps us to do that. I know too that this philosophy was not original. Thornton Wilder crafted *Our Town* and William Carlos Williams revolutionized American poetry around much the same concept. For me, however, it will always be John Boy Walton who brought personal writing into my life and made me realize that the ordinary things and everyday people are what good writing is all about.

The power of the journal struck me again later in life when I read *Be True to Your School* by Bob Greene. The book is a diary that the journalist kept as a high school senior in 1964. He kept it as an exercise to improve his writing skills, but it turned out to be much more. Although Greene's senior year was more than a decade before mine, the feelings and events were remarkably similar to what I experienced and remain contemporary as well. In his preface, Greene expresses what I suspect anyone who keeps a diary will find: "It has been like stepping into a daily time machine; I have been able to walk away from the world I live in now, and walk in to 1964. That year was a very special time in my life."

We need to appreciate the moments and as writers to capture them. In *Dead Poets Society* Robin Williams' Mr. Keating challenges his students to "seize the day" which is what writers must do. Journals and diaries remind us to stop the world and preserve the day or the moment.

"Goodbye My Friend"

Why does it always seem that the people that have the most impact on our lives are gone in an instant? When my friend Gary said, "We will talk more when I have more time," we both knew that they would be the last words we would share. He was getting ready to shower, to put more affairs in order, to finalize some plans. When our phone call ended, I would return to my daily routine in a day like many others, and he would continue to make the most of his remaining days. All the while, the numbing morphine was already coursing through his veins, easing the pain that he had turned to meaning as an activist and exemplar.

We knew that there would be no more time. That during the few minutes we spoke, we said the things that, left unspoken, might have led to regrets later on. So we thanked each other for things like friendship and love and admiration. Things that, I suppose by their very existence between two people, need not be mentioned, but that are gratefully acknowledged all the same.

After we spoke, I returned to my empty classroom, the one in which we had shared morning talks of the students we both worked with in our professional lives and of our lives beyond the classroom. I rummaged through my desk to find a tape of a little known Linda Ronstadt song written by Karla Bonoff. I played the cassette. The song is called "Goodbye

My Friend" and begins, "Oh, we never know where life will take us. I know it's just a ride on the wheel. And we never know when death will shake us, and we wonder how it will feel."

I suppose there is a certain comfort in knowing that your time is limited and in being able to plan for some closure in one's relationships and personal matters. Many found it surprising, even approaching morbid, that Gary was an active participant in planning his own memorial service. This though is not at all uncommon in times when our modern plague is taking our finest writers, performers, artists, and in Gary's case, educators.

It was both comforting and troubling to me, as well as at least a bit ironic, that when we spoke, he sounded like himself, same upbeat tone, familiar inflections. I rewound the tape and played it again, its lyrics seeming to fill a void: "So goodbye my friend. I know I'll never see you again. But the time together through all the years will take away these tears. It's O.K. now. Goodbye my friend."

Gary was fortunate to have the unflagging and unconditional support of his family, friends, and colleagues through every step of his ordeal. He seemed at peace with his decisions and comforted by the opportunity to plan his goodbyes. To be able to move on with the same dignity with which he lived.

I played the song once more. "Life so fragile and love so pure. We can't hold on but we try. We watch how quickly it disappears and we never know why. But I'm O.K. now. Goodbye my friend. You can go now. Goodbye my friend."

Shortly thereafter, I attended Gary's memorial service. As people spoke of him, his accomplishments, and the difference he made for so many in half a lifetime, I learned a lot about what makes a life meaningful.

~

Keep a diary for one week. Write only things you feel, remember, or think about. Don't write about things you do. Try to seize a moment.

A Brief Introduction to Time Travel

From H.G. Wells' classic 1895 novel *The Time Machine* to Marty McFly trying to save his own life by uniting his parents in the 1985 Robert Zemeckis film *Back to the Future*, time travel has fascinated generations. For writers, time travel must been viewed as an actuality. We can return to long gone times, change events, meet our ancestors, and visit far away places.

Writers as a breed are able to see beyond the boundaries instituted by mankind and the human mind. Just as George Burns and Gary Shandling in their television shows broke down the "fourth" wall and spoke directly to the audience, writers are able to ignore the arbitrary and contrived boundaries of time and space and become one with the past.

Let's begin with a discussion about the physics of time travel. While it would be valuable to a writer to have the blind faith to believe that we can travel in time, let's cater to human instinct for a moment and ponder the obvious question. Is time travel possible?

If you could travel at a speed approximating the speed of light, time would stop once you finally achieve the speed of light. Once your speed passes the speed of light, time would go backwards, allowing you to enter the realm of negative time, the past. Black holes seem to play a role as well. These are dense celestial objects that pull time and space to a breaking point. Wormholes then connect black holes to one another, but they do not exist for long and are only about the size of an atom. Got all that? Me neither. Let's look at some more practical aspects of time travel.

Time travel is founded on a paradox. If you were to go back in time and kill your great grandfather, you would not exist because he would not have lived to produce the generations that followed. However, if you did this, you would not have existed in the first place to go back and do the killing. One theory that is floated about to explain this suggests that a parallel universe would develop so that there would then be universes where you both exist and do not exist. More and more layers of universes would develop as necessary to prevent a time traveler from changing the course of history. This also addresses the question as to whether or not we could be a part of the past or would just be viewing images of what was as if watching a movie. Theories suggest that certain things in the past are "set" and that a time traveler's attempt to alter them would ultimately be thwarted in order to preserve the natural order of the universe.

Now, let's move beyond the theoretical. We all constantly censor our experiences. We focus on different aspects of a situation than others there at the same time might focus in on. Suppose three people approach the food court in a mall from different directions. At the point where their paths would merge is a table where a young couple sits having a rather loud disagreement. The three shoppers who approach will notice different things. Some will focus on the male, other the female. For one of the shoppers something about the clothing the two wear might seem significant. For another it might be the words of the arguing couple. Each of the three observers will return home and relay the situation to a friend. There would at that point be three different versions of the story. Each version would be accurate to the person telling it. Does this not represent the formation of three parallel universes? Each of the three people (and potentially dozens of others) still has his or her own version of the experience and no version changes any of the others.

Writers need to be able to suspend limitations, such as the boundaries of time and space, and create parallel universes.

Summer 2000.

It was the first time I had been back to Wilkes-Barre, Pennsylvania since my grandmother's death five years earlier. My son was seven at the time and we took the trip to visit the cemetery where my grandparents are buried and to catch up with some relatives. Some of the places I had always gone to were the same; others were different, while others no longer existed at all. Memories came flooding back. I jotted down notes as we drove around the areas where I had taken my grandmother so many times. The memories went deeper still. I was transported back not only to the years approaching her death at eighty-nine, when I was in my thirties, but also to the summers I would spend there as a child when both she and my grandfather were alive. The trip triggered a trilogy of poems, "Living," "Living and Dying," and "Living Again" in which I strived to capture the times we had spent together over several decades. It was an amazing feeling. I was not visiting the past, but rather, I had the sensation that I was reliving it with a red 1991 Chevy Cavalier as a time machine.

Spring 2004.

The human mind is a warehouse filled with memories of everything we have ever experienced. The slightest random prompt can be remarkably effective in bringing those memories out of storage and into the present. It had been thirty years, since my first, and only, visit to Philadelphia. It was a three or four day eighth grade class trip which we requested, since so many of us had already been to Washington, DC, the traditional destination of the middle school graduating class. In the ensuing years I remembered how much we enjoyed the trip and some of the attractions we visited. Thirty years later, possibly to the day, my friend Joe and I, along with my ten-year-old son, went to Philadelphia to plan a trip for the middle school classes I was then teaching. Joe, a colleague, had grown up outside of the city and served as the tour guide for the day. As we walked the streets, visited the sites, ate cheese steaks, and mapped out our routes around the city, I was thirteen again. We walked past a Holiday Inn and suddenly I remembered the room several friends and I had shared there and that tennis player Bobby Riggs, a guest that week on the old *Mike Douglas* talk show, was staying there at the same time. I remembered Betsy Ross' house and the other historical venues and the teachers and friends I had walked those streets with three decades earlier. The places where we ate, the conversations we had, and even the voice and words of the old man doing scientific demonstrations for us at the Franklin Institute all came flooding back. The memories became that much stronger, that much more precious, and were joined by a new set thirty years newer.

~

Write your own explanation of the time travel paradox. Don't worry about being scientifically correct.

Yours Too is a Wonderful Life

"You see George, you really had a wonderful life," explains Clarence Oddbody, angel second class, to George Bailey in Frank Capra's 1946 film classic *It's a Wonderful Life*. Bailey of course is the despondent building and loan officer played by Jimmy Stewart who feels he has done nothing of significance in or with his life. In the enduring holiday favorite he is shown by his guardian angel that in fact all of the little, seemingly unimportant, things that go unnoticed are life's important moments after all.

Whether teaching a workshop, college class, or just looking for a topic to write about, I think about this. So often a student or even a seasoned veteran writer will say, "I have nothing to write about." There is a tendency to believe that in order to have something to write about and to reach the pinnacle of the writing process, publication, one needs to have experienced unique and remarkable events. That need not be the case. We are the sum total of all of our experiences. All we have done, every age we have been, every person we have met, remain a part of us and provide all that is needed to always have something to write about.

Writers, both aspiring and established, frequently fear for their next idea, wondering if they will ever find the elusive "big story." The truth is that we have all lived the big stories. A first kiss and the inevitable first breakup. Winning the big game and striking out in the bottom of the ninth. Hitting every note at your first recital. Each moment that has given us pleasure and each that has given us pain is a story waiting to be told.

I had been working with sixteen-year-old Katie for about a year, tutoring her in various subjects. We had reached the point where it was time to begin a more formal writing program. I asked her to make a list of good and bad things that have happened to her, of things she likes, of things she feels she might be able to say something about.

A week later this intelligent, sensitive young woman who

I knew had an ability to notice and appreciate little things that seem trivial to others, had little more than a blank sheet of paper and was certain that she had nothing significant to write about. "I couldn't think of anything good. Nothing good has ever happened to me." By "good" she was thinking of important, influential, earth shattering events, not the small personal things that make up daily living. Not the personal, painful things we like to keep hidden.

I asked her to forget about how important the things were that she puts on her list, explaining that I had published articles about such personal and trivial things as my favorite radio station from when I was growing up, my favorite television show, a twenty-year-old date book, a young girl's bat mitzvah, and donating blood for the first time. Katie then came up with a list that included things like: I got a computer for Christmas, I got 100 on a test, my mom died when I was five, volleyball, ice skating, and family events like an illness and a remarriage.

She then picked the item on her list that she felt she had the most to say about – her mother's death. She began to think of various angles the piece could take like what it felt like, how it still affects her, what to expect, of how others respond in such situations. What she selected obviously was not a trivial event, but one that was more than a decade old, so did not seem relevant to her as a writer in the here and now.

Next I asked if she would like to write an article about it and try to get it published. She agreed but added, "I could not write it about myself, but I could pretend it was for one of those magazines where someone writes in with a problem and they give advice about it." I told her that she could approach it that way but that it might be easier to write it in the first person and then change it to the third person later.

The next week she had the first draft of an article that flowed with concise, moving prose like her opening, "At the age of five everything is supposed to be fun and games…but what happens when it is time to teach children about something tragic, something that they will hardly understand?" Katie still was not sure, however, that it was important enough. "I came up with a couple of memories, but I can't think of any others." I responded that she should stop worrying about whether her ideas were "worthy" of being put down on paper. If they were part of her, they were important enough.

She wrote of her touching memories with grace and style. They were small personal memories that she had thought not significant enough to write an article about, yet significant enough to be clear in her mind eleven years after her mother's death. She wrote of the book her mom gave her to keep track of the days until she would return home from hospital stays, of lying in bed together watching *Little House on the Prairie*, of her mom taking her picture on the first day of kindergarten, of her singing her to sleep with "Silent Night," and of the day she lost her forever.

Her article appeared in a national magazine and she came to know that she has stories to tell. Her article, incidentally, remained in the first person and it is hard to imagine it any other way. She knows her topics need not be unique or have an obvious impact on the world. They just need to be part of her.

We all have little things that we can recall so well that are more universal than we might think: The drive-in movie theater that is now a strip mall. The corner grocery where everyone knew everyone else. The shiny silver diner that is now a fast food outlet. That feeling in the pit of your stomach when you made your first phone call to a member of the opposite sex. We just need to tell our stories with honesty, clarity, and emotion. Do not embellish, and at the same time, do not hold back. We need to trust our experiences and encourage others to do the same. After all, Katie was but one of many students I have worked with, yet this essay was only possible because she is now part of my sum total of experiences and has touched my life and made it better without even knowing it. Just like George Bailey learned from Clarence, "Strange isn't it? Each person's life touches so many other lives."

"Dad Already Received His Father's Day Gift"

My son Justin Matthew is almost two years old, and his

favorite movie is *Angels in the Outfield*. He stands up at the appropriate times and waves his arms and quotes the film's catch phrase, "It could happen." He likes the idea that Father's Day is approaching, offering with a giggle that he and my wife, Marie, have a "'prise" in store for me.

This year, his gift will still be something my wife picks out, but I know that before long, he will be presenting me with wonderful treasures like cards cut and pasted from colored construction paper, boxes made from Popsicle sticks glued together, and outlandish neckties that I will wear with pride.

When I first saw the shadowy images on the ultrasound screen that would develop into a child, I was not at all certain what kind of father I would be. Parenthood looked easy from a distance to those of us who grew up in the media generation.

All Robert Young ever needed was a sports jacket with patches on the elbows to set Princess, Bud, and Kitten on the straight and narrow. Ward Cleaver and Mike Brady had their heart-to-heart talks and occasional stern looks. From Ozzie Nelson to Andy Taylor, from *My Little Margie* to *My Three Sons*, the moral lessons were neatly delivered in thirty-minute segments.

Suddenly, though, I was faced with the responsibility of finding the real-life key to raising a well-adjusted, self-assured, morally upright child. I posed a question to several dozen seventh grade students: "What is the most important thing parents can do for their children?" Their answers were remarkably similar. They were concise, yet insightful and filled with youthful optimism. They were also wonderfully devoid of material wishes. "Help them through hard times." "Show them they love them." "Let them know they care and are around." "Talk to them." "Support and educate them." "Have respect for them."

Perhaps my son enjoys emulating angels because they do for people exactly what my seventh-graders suggest parents should do: love, help, care, support, educate, respect. All in all, not a bad set of guidelines to think about on Father's Day, and every day.

Perhaps then, all of our children will grow up echoing the

sentiments of one twelve-year-old who said of her parents, "They are the best and closest friends I will ever have. I trust them and value their thoughts."

Like Justin likes to say, "It could happen."

~

Write about a personal experience that you do not think is important enough to write about.

Keeping the Oral Tradition Alive

The obituary in *The New York Times* saying that Columbia University professor Wallace Gray had died of a heart attack at age 74 took me by surprise. I had always taken for granted that he was one of those people who had been there forever and always would be, no less than the statue of Alma Mater sitting on the steps of Low Library.

One of the world's foremost authorities on James Joyce, Dr. Gray was already a legend on the Columbia campus when I arrived as an insecure freshman in the fall of 1978. His course "Eliot, Joyce, and Pound" was always filled to lecture hall capacity, and he would offer, not as braggadocio, but as a matter of fact and honesty, "I know all there is to know about *Ulysses* and am going to teach you all of it."

The confidence. The mastery. The ability to be intellectual without distancing himself as an intellect. Would I, I wondered, ever know enough about anything to teach it to others? As the semester progressed, we discussed a pending term paper. I expressed an interest in experimenting with a creative exercise like Joyce did, when he used Homer's *The Odyssey* as the framework for *Ulysses*. Professor Gray encouraged me to do so and gave me the freedom to try. It was a crude attempt to be sure as I tried to write experimental fiction, not really even knowing what the genre was all about. Instead of Leopold Bloom wandering through Dublin, I had a New York City cab driver on an odyssey of self-discovery. Just having a renowned professor, however, give me the opportunity to do something in academia that I had never done before, taught me far more than writing any research paper about James Joyce would have.

A couple of years later, as a senior, I felt fortunate to be accepted into his small seminar course. We studied *Ulysses*, each taking two chapters and presenting our research based analysis to the rest of the group. I was excited and honored to be included in the seminar, which also included a bright young classmate named George Stephanopoulos, but then the magnitude of the task struck me. How could I possibly find something to say that was original? Something Dr. Gray did not know? My turn came and I ran through my chapters, citing reference materials and guiding the rest of the group in a choppy manner at best, still not sure I would ever know enough about anything to teach it. At one point I offered a personal interpretation of what seemed an inconsequential line in the novel. Dr. Gray stopped me and asked if the point I had just made was an original idea. I said that it was and he was impressed. The insecure freshman had become a senior who found a thought that the expert had not yet come upon.

That moment was certainly one of many that had been long forgotten in Dr. Gray's distinguished career, but was a career defining one for me. I could, after all, know enough about something to teach it. Years went by, indeed a century came to an end, and I found myself in the role of veteran teacher. I had taught high school, middle school, and as surprising as it would have been to the insecure freshman, English at the college level. I sent Dr. Gray a note reminiscing about the seminar and of how the things I learned from him have over time been incorporated into my own teaching, things like allowing students to be individuals and to take chances, and of how being honest about who you are and how you approach what you teach are the best ways to reach students.

He wrote back, remembering our time together, and still encouraging and supporting, "Given what you wrote to me about relationships between teacher and text and teacher and student, I am confident that you are a marvelous teacher. Besides, given your enthusiasms for life, literature, and other people, how could you not be?"

As I looked at that letter, side by side with his obituary, and a mimeographed invitation to an end of semester wine party he had given us after the seminar, it saddened me to realize that he would not be part of the campus forever. Then I thought again of the freedom he gave me to learn in my own way, and the encouragement he gave me in his seminar. He made me realize the value of recognizing even the smallest contribution, and that I had the ability to contribute to the body of knowledge we call academia. I thought of these things and I knew that I was mistaken. He lives on through what I do every day, and maybe that is what teaching is all about.

In addition to Dr. Gray, I was fortunate enough to have another professor who had a profound influence on me. I remember when I read "The Circus." It was the fall of 1980. I knew little about poetry, less about modern poetry, and still less about writing poetry. It was my junior year and I had registered for Modern Poetry taught by Kenneth Koch. I soon discovered that this spectacled, curly haired teacher, who showed occasional tendencies toward the stereotypical "absent minded professor" was not only a founding member of the renowned New York School of Poets (along with Frank O'Hara, John Ashbery, and James Schuyler) but was also an instructor who would provide me with an inspiration that, as a teacher and writer, serves me to this day.

After a session early in the semester, I combed New York City bookstores and found a slim volume of Koch's poems titled of *The Art Love*. Between its covers I found "The Circus," a reflective poem that makes reference to an earlier poem of his with the same title. In the later poem he writes of his friends and, in an ending passage that haunts me as strongly now as when I first read it, of his late wife Janice, and their time in Paris. It was a revelation to me that poems could be written in such a conversational style and still be moving and powerful. It was a further revelation that mentioning one's friends and loved ones and inspirations was acceptable too. While it took many more years of reading and writing for me to feel a true intimacy with the poetic process, the shroud of mystery that had previously covered it had been lifted. Moreover, Kenneth Koch and I became writing partners forever more.

No, Kenneth Koch and I never wrote anything together. Indeed, except for a couple of brief notes we exchanged in the ensuing years in which he expressed his pleasure in having been a good influence, I was little more than another of the thousands of students who passed through his classroom. Still, even after his death, we remain collaborators in a very real sense. Everyone we have ever read or have been inspired by is a part of the unique voice writers strive to develop. I look at my own poems and can see his influence, just as I can look at my own newspaper columns and see the bits and pieces that I have incorporated through years of reading Bob Greene, Pete Hamill, Mike Lupica, Anna Quindlen, Frank Rich, and Mike Royko. This is not to suggest that I place my work on the same level of these influential and widely read columnists. It is merely to point out that those we read become part of what we write.

***

In 1997 I had the opportunity to interview folk singer Pete Seeger. One of the topics we discussed was the oral tradition. "My father said that a song printed in a book is like a picture of a bird in flight," he explained. "The song is changing before and it is changing after it was published in the book; the bird was flapping its wings before the shutter clicked and it kept on flapping its wings after the camera clicked." He has seen this process take place with his own music. "Hardly a single one of my songs has been recorded as I wrote it. 'Where Have All the Flowers Gone' – I just wrote three verses. A young fellow at summer camp gave it more rhythm and added two verses, and that's the way Peter, Paul and Mary picked it up, and the Kingston Trio got it, and Marlene Dietrich took it around the world. She gave it a very German translation. I hardly ever sing my original version. The same thing, he explained, happened with 'If I Had a Hammer.' Peter, Paul and Mary changed my tune and then it took off." Certainly one of the most revered performers of his time, Seeger does not put much value on things like awards. He is proudest of being a "link in a chain" of people who are carrying on the ideas that he learned from Woody Guthrie. He likes that it is possible to, "Put new words to an old tune and tell the story of what's going on in these modern times."

As writers we are all links in a chain. After attending a Harry Chapin tribute concert, my son and I were listening to some of his songs in the car on the way home. I had been listening to Chapin's music for over thirty years, but revisiting the lyrics from a writer's perspective, I realized that his influence was present in my own poetry. For the first time I felt his song "We Were Three" in the themes of my poem "The Last Automat." His "Pretzel Man" could have been in the same neighborhood where my "Twisting Unicorns" is set. My "Different Worlds" shares an underlying theme with Chapin's "Taxi." All of us, links in a chain.

~

Make copies of at least three pieces of your writing. Give them to five other people to read. Ask them to pass them on.

A Brief Introduction to Coal Mining

Not many people would have predicted the phenomenal success and popularity of the ever-growing catalogue of titles in the *Chicken Soup for the Soul* series of anthologies. They are not built on thrilling plot lines, celebrity sensationalism, or even persuasive marketing techniques. These collections of inspirational anecdotes have been embraced by millions of readers because they draw upon the ordinary experiences of ordinary people. Fewer still might have forecast success for Frank McCourt's *Angela's Ashes* and Mitch Albom's *Tuesdays with Morrie* in times when John Grisham and Stephen King were the dominant names on the best seller lists, yet the aforementioned memoirs both became the type of blockbusters authors and publishing houses dream about.

Memoir is a powerful, emotional, and, above all, highly personal channel through which one can harvest material for virtually every genre of writing, attain a heightened self-awareness, and achieve a cathartic effect. I have always been guided by the philosophy that we are the sum total of our experiences and that everything we have done and every person we have met remain a part of who we are and affect every experience that follows. We need, as writers, to access those experiences in order to examine their role in our lives.

A lifetime is a series of random events that somehow become a unified tapestry of people, places, and events, which we refer to as "self." By developing this heightened self-awareness, writers become more confident and willing to share their work and develop a storehouse of material that can be used for personal essays, poems, plays, and fiction. In order to reclaim the memories that lie buried deep beneath the surface of our conscious minds, we need to apply a mining process, an unearthing of the layers of self upon which all subsequent layers sit.

In strip-mining, workers remove layers of the earth to

unveil the valuable coal resting below. As each layer is carted away, that which was hidden eventually becomes the surface. We can apply this same excavation process as writers seeking the hidden treasures of our pasts. Cataloguing one's memories is an effective way to free others that are related, but often deeply hidden. It may sound like a daunting task, but one of the best ways to free yourself as a writer is to recreate your entire life as part of your daily writing.

Get a notebook that you are comfortable with. Write only on the right hand sides of the pages leaving the facing pages blank. Make a list of the segments of your life. A good start might be pre-school memories, followed by a section for each year of school, memories outside of the school setting, holidays, friendships, illnesses, jobs, scouts or other clubs, sports, summers, adolescence, and so forth. Then for each, do a stream of consciousness writing exercise in which you write down everything you can remember about the topic. Do not worry about how accurate sequences of events or dates are just let the information keep flowing. Within the writing ask yourself questions about how your life might have been different had your decisions been different from those you made. Then try to answer those questions.

Periodically go back to the memories you have jotted down. They will inevitably jar further remembrances. Write those down those new memories on the facing pages that you left blank. This should be an ongoing process which will provide a wealth of ideas, topics, and anecdotes on which to base future pieces of writing. You will begin to see connections among events that earlier you might not have realized.

To help prompt the memory, look to anything that contains fragments of your past. Look at photos that you and your family have, reread letters you have received and tucked away in a shoe box. Discarded calendars, address books, and appointment books as well as school and medical records all contain hints of who we are and where we came from.

My old friend Cliff, upon reading a couple of my poetry collections said to me, "I'll bet everyone tells you he or she is a poet. It must be frustrating." Not at all. Everyone *is* a poet;

a writer is in there somewhere. My job is to help unearth that writer.

"Another Look at Coal Mining"

The dirtiest work I ever did was summers spent in a lumberyard during my teenage years. Loading two by fours and bags of cement into pickup trucks could not come close to what my grandfather endured as a child working in the coal mines of Northeastern Pennsylvania. I never gave much thought to what he used to say to me with a laugh, "If grandma and I never met, you would not be here" until one summer when everything took on a new perspective.

I can still feel the layers of rock above and below me as I crawled across the subterranean ledge, not much wider or higher that I was at the time. It was like an elongated coffin or a tunnel for the electric trains taken out only at Christmas then returned to the attic. Water flowed below and stalactites hung above. The air was far from fresh and sunlight was a distant memory. The rappel down from the surface was fun, but the rest of the spelunking experience was one I was glad to have done, but not anxious to repeat.

That was about a quarter century before the mining accident of the summer of 2002 and the feeling of claustrophobia, of having no control over the yards and yards of earth above, can still rush back in a flash. My underground experience lasted less than an hour. I can only imagine the feelings of those nine Pennsylvania coal miners, trapped for more than three days in the dark, dank underground in a place reserved for the underworld mythology of unclaimed souls.

As I sat, anxious about their fate, looking for the all too few updates on the twenty-four hour news channels, I clung to the fading hope that a miracle would bring them to the surface. I thought of how if a similar incident had taken place during the early decades of the twentieth century I might not exist to be watching this event unfold or to be writing this.

As a child my grandfather, after whom I am named, worked as a breaker boy in the coal mines of Pittston,

Pennsylvania. For less than a dollar a day he would separate the worthless chunks of rock and earth from the valuable coal. Eventually he moved farther into the mining process and farther into the earth. Ultimately, seeing what mining did to the lives of some coworkers, he left the mines for work as a laborer, a truck driver, and a long career in retail sales. He left with his life intact, though in the long term, not his lungs.

The days went on and even with the technology and innovations available today, it seemed that optimism for the nine trapped miners was more political posturing and wistfulness than reality. The cable networks continued to offer more talking head shots than coverage from the site. In times when we are surrounded by unhappy endings, we rarely stop to think about the arbitrary nature of our existence, of how any event could have prevented it and of how any could take it away.

As Saturday morning became afternoon, I watched my son play with his friends at his birthday party, alive because my grandfather had been, and wondered it the trapped miners would see their children's next birthdays. Would prayers for the miners make the more and more improbable rescue take place?

After midnight while we were getting ready for bed, the headlines flashed on the television screen. All nine miners were alive. My wife and I sat, dozing on and off through the night as one by one each man was raised to the surface from his temporary tomb 240 feet below.

Maybe a miracle. Maybe fate. Maybe a combination of faith, luck, and divine inspiration. Whatever it was, it is nice to see things work out just as you hope for every once in a while.

~

Start working on the "recreate your life" exercise described in this section. Get a blank journal that you find appealing and spend a little time every day adding to the collection of memories that will emerge. Do not censor yourself.

Serendipity

Serendipity is one of my favorite words. I like the sound of it and the movie that uses it as its title. I especially like it because as a writer it reminds me over and over that you never know where you might find inspiration, and that while hard work and dedication are still the best principles to guide a writer, there is no need to discount the role that sheer luck might play.

It was serendipitous that I ended up learning about teaching and poetry from Kenneth Koch. I applied to Columbia University because I wanted the opportunity to live in New York City for four years and I liked Columbia's campus the best of the schools I visited. I registered for his class not because I knew who he was, and how important a figure in the literary world he was, but because it fit into my schedule. Though I was little more than another face in a large lecture hall crowd, the two semesters I spent with him changed my life.

One of the biggest venues I have been published in is *The New York Daily News*. To appear in the same newspaper that has featured some of my literary "heroes" such as Mike Lupica and Pete Hamill was an exciting experience. It was also not one that I sought out, but rather one that serendipitously found me.

My friend Rob said to me one day, "I was riding the subway today, reading *The Daily News* over someone's shoulder and I saw your byline." I thought that was amazing and a tremendous ego trip, but also a bit puzzling since I had never written anything for the paper. He told me a little of what the article was about and I recognized it as a piece I had sold quite some time earlier to *College Bound Magazine*, in which it had already appeared.

I called *The Daily News* and was connected to the special sections editor who told me that they had purchased the rights to run the piece from *College Bound*. I asked her if she ever used freelancers and she agreed to read some further clips. That led to several new sales to the *Daily News*, a newspaper that I have been reading all of my life.

As we get older we become more introspective as we look for answers to life's questions. The answers to those questions, however, often come from where we least expect it. Serendipity.

As the son of a Jewish mother, according to the laws of Judaism, I am Jewish. Growing up Catholic, however, my knowledge of Judaism was largely limited to my grandmother's occasional lighting of candles and her matzo ball soup simmering on the stove of her long gone apartment in the Bronx.

I had always been church-going religious, but I never had a particularly religious experience. Even meeting hundreds of priests as a staff member of a Catholic newspaper before pursuing a career in education and freelance writing, there was something missing. It never crossed my mind that a Jewish religious service would be where I would begin to find the special feeling of being part of something bigger and more spiritual that religion should be all about.

I was invited to attend my first ever Bat Mitzvah. I have never particularly enjoyed formal ceremonies like weddings, confirmations, and so forth, and have an even stronger aversion to Saturday morning commitments. Thus, an invitation to spend a Saturday listening to two and a half hours of singing and praying in Hebrew, which I do not understand a word of, was not my idea of a welcomed addition to my social calendar. I accepted, however, and much to my surprise, found a path to what I had been seeking.

The young woman being called to Torah was a student of mine in seventh grade English. As I listened to the teaching she shared and took in everything happening in the ceremony, I felt something I had not previously encountered in a religious service. There was everywhere a sense of family and of community. I began to feel that in my own parish, in my own family.

Her teaching that morning was based on the idea that we will all have to justify our words in heaven one day. She spoke of the danger of gossip and how the tongue's natural position is at rest, thus indicating that we consciously chose what we say.

Later when her rabbi spoke of Andrea, he described her just as I would have from knowing her in class. He said that she has a presence that brightens a room on even a dreary morning when everyone else would have preferred to remain in bed. It struck me that rabbi means teacher and that somehow there was a connection of purpose in what we do and that perhaps the student is the best teacher after all is said and done.

It took a young girl singing and praying on a Saturday morning in a foreign tongue to help me realize that we need not look too far to realize that we are a part of something bigger and more spiritual than ourselves. Happenstance? Fate? Luck? Serendipity? I don't know what to call it, but I do know that as writers, we should welcome it and allow it to guide us as much as anything else.

***

The first poem I ever wrote that I felt was "good" or at least that made me fee that I had some talent to develop in that area, happened quite by accident. I was in Central Park in New York City and an artist was doing sketches of people in charcoal. It was fascinating to see the sketches develop and to then see them side by side with the subjects who would pay him a few crumpled dollars and walk away with a masterpiece rolled in tissue paper. I thought about how he was giving them a lasting memory of him, but that he would not remember any of them. These and many other images came together to become "Charcoal Drawings in the Park" which appeared in two of my books and in several magazines.

~

Make a list of coincidences you have experienced. How might your life, or your view of life, be different had those chance occurrences not happened?

Crosspollination of the Arts

One night about a month into the semester of a college Basic Writing course I was teaching, one of the students came up to me after class saying that he was perplexed about how to gain confidence as a writer. He felt that teachers over the years did not like his writing but never really gave him a reason above and beyond the grammar and spelling corrections they scribbled on his papers. He seemed almost defeated. He wanted to write well but did not even know what questions he wanted answered. We began to talk about process and of how reading good writers can help one become a better writer. I mentioned how I learned about poetry and began to develop my own style through the methods used by Kenneth Koch when I was a student of his years earlier at Columbia.

I explained how by using imitation and trying to create original works in the styles of the masters who came before us, bits and pieces start to merge and your own voice eventually emerges. Almost like in the cartoons when a light bulb suddenly appears over someone's head when the great idea is born, the student said, "Wait a minute. I am a musician and that's exactly how I learned to play music. I listened to earlier versions and performances and went from there." Exactly. I liken good writing to jazz. You can take chances and can break the rules, yet something artistic and beautiful can still emerge.

Early in life I accepted my fate as the one in my family lacking musical ability. By age ten I had barely mastered "Lady of Spain" on the accordion and left the performing to my two brothers who both became professional musicians. My father fronted a neighborhood band in the Bronx during the years that bridged the big band era and the street corner doo-wop sound. My inability to carry a tune has not kept music from being a major influence and inspiration in my life.

Growing up, the *American Top 40* radio program with Casey Kasem was always like an original cast record for my life. I knew the national survey positions of each song as well as the New York positions on the WABC survey counted down each week by disc jockey Cousin Brucie. Now when I glance at the lists published regularly in the newspaper, I am lucky to recognize two or three artists' names, never mind the songs. Paul McCartney's "Band on the Run" and the Hues Corporation's "Rock the Boat" can still instantly transport me back to eighth grade, the year when I first started to become who I was rather than who I thought others thought I should be. It was not until years later that I even heard of self-esteem theories. The bridge from high school to college was Billy Joel's *The Stranger*, Meat Loaf's *Bat Out of Hell*, and the soundtrack from *Saturday Night Fever*. Listening to those albums or other songs from various time periods in my life never fails to provide inspiration.

The connections among the arts are compelling and motivating. The New York School of Poets, Koch along with John Ashbery, Frank O'Hara, and James Schuyler worked to formalize the interconnected nature of the arts. They collaborated with artists such as Larry Rivers and Jane Freilicher to form a group of innovative and groundbreaking practitioners of the creative arts that David Lehman dubbed "the last avant-garde" in his book *The Last Avant-Garde: The Making of the New York School of Poets.*

Kerin, a young artist, was among the most talented members of one of my poetry workshops one semester. We discussed the similarities between her writing and her painting, both important in her life. "It is a way for me to get my feelings and emotions out rather than keeping them inside, which is what I tend to do." While it is not surprising that both activities are inspired by the emotions and experiences in her life, I found it interesting that the physical processes of creating a painting and a poem were, for her, similar as well. "I always have trouble both starting a poem and starting a painting. First, I outline my picture to be painted by creating a rough sketch. Then I fill it in with colors, etc. It is the same with poetry. First, I create an initial draft that comes to my head, and later I fill in the blanks and alter it."

She continues explaining the creative process saying, "Once I get past starting a project, I focus my attention solely on that project and nothing else. That way, I am able to get out all of the feeling and emotion that I want to without being interrupted. After I paint or I write, I always feel a sense of accomplishment and relief as I have just released something into the world that otherwise would have been held inside of me, for no one to see."

***

The third section of my book *Composite Sketches* is called "K-tel Presents Believe in Poetry." It is comprised of poems inspired by the songs I loved as I was growing up. K-tel was a record company that would put out compilations of songs and *Believe in Music* was one of the company's first releases. I find that listening to the songs later in my life is much the same as when I first heard them. They still sound fresh and still evoke feelings and images. I find it sad that some of the personal connections that people make with music are not as common or as strong or as long lasting as was once the case. In the decades since "Video Killed the Radio Star" with the advent of MTV and music videos, an entire generation has grown up content to be shown what a song is supposed to be about, rather than letting free-form images develop and fill the mind.

~

Make a CD or tape compilation of your favorite songs from a special time period in your life. Use stream of consciousness to write while you listen. Look at a painting or photograph that you find particularly haunting. Write what comes to your mind.

Calligriotherapy

In bibliotherapy literature is used as a means to deal with painful situations in life. Stories in which characters deal with hard times similar to those of the reader can provide a sense of support and of being less alone. This should come as no surprise. One of the basic tenets preached in fiction writing workshops is to create characters that people can relate to. Writers are taught to seek universal truths in their work. Writing too has a therapeutic affect. It can help us cope, learn, grow, accept, and move on.

Calligriotherapy will appear on a computer screen underlined in red. It is a word that I believe I created and hope to eventually coax into Standard English. Writing as a means of self-examination and as a way of dealing with stressful times is hardly a new concept. People have long kept diaries and journals for those reasons and beyond. We have a human desire to ponder the "whys" of our lives, to clarify our values and morals, to resolve inner conflicts. I do not look at caligriotherapy as armchair psychology, but rather as learning how to be introspective and to move closer to self-awareness. If I were to write a definition for Webster's, I might suggest: Calligriotherapy-(noun) the process of writing about one's experiences to encourage self-examination through introspection.

As I look back at many of the newspaper columns that I have published over the years, I realize that I have, unwittingly, used them as a way of accepting the deaths of and memorializing people I have lost in my life. One was written following the deaths of two special people in my life the same year I had lost my paternal grandmother; two others looked back at the moments and kindnesses shared in daily life.

"Fond Images Help Keep Old Friends Alive"

One of my favorite songs, one that gives me that philosophy to live by feeling is "Circle" by Harry Chapin. The lyrics in part are, "All my life's a circle, but I can't tell you why. The seasons spinning 'round again, the years keep on rolling by." I like it because it says that nothing important to us really leaves us for good. This feeling that we are the sum of our experiences was passed on to a new generation through "The Circle of Life" in *The Lion King*.

I found comfort in this concept, that those we come in contact with remain a part of us, upon opening a local newspaper and finding that two very significant people in my life had passed on. They were not among those I kept in regular contact with but for various reasons were always there, always part of the world I exist in.

As a child growing up in Carmel, New York, walking "up street" to visit Kurtz's newspaper store was symbolic of an ever increasing independence. As childhood became adolescence and adolescence turned to the college years, Joe Greene was a constant behind the counter at Kurtz's in an ever changing world that progressively reached beyond Carmel's borders. I can still recall that gruff façade giving way to embarrassment whenever we kids remembered his birthday or some other occasion. To Joe, we were forever "lads" or "young 'uns."

At a stage in life when most people begin looking toward retiring from a career, Gerard Mergardt embarked on a new one. I have always felt honored to have had him for a high school English teacher and have often included his example among my reasons for becoming an English teacher.

I can recall a time or two stopping by his home on a whim after his retirement and after my graduation and being welcomed with a modesty that almost said, "What did I do to be remembered so fondly by a former student?" Our paths would continue to cross through occasional chance meetings at the bank or via inquiries through mutual friends.

Some people just seem to have an effect on others whom they come in contact with that, even long after their final meeting, leaves a sense of loss equal to that of one's own family members. My grandmother died in January at the age of eighty-nine. Just as I still find myself planning one more of our lunch dates and ritual visits to relatives throughout Northeastern Pennsylvania, I know for a long time to come I will expect to hear Joe Greene's voice from the back of the store where he would cook his breakfast on his little hot plate. I know too that I will continue to expect Mr. Mergardt to stroll out of Putnam County Savings Bank in his patented dignified style.

These are images that will forever be part of who I am and, I like to think, will keep these old friends among us for a little while longer.

"We All Have a Morrie in Our Lives"

In *Tuesdays with Morrie,* Mitch Albom quotes his dying teacher, friend, and mentor Morrie Schwartz as saying of death, "As long as we can love each other, and remember the feeling of love we had, we can die without ever really going away. All the love you created is still there. All the memories are still there. You live on in the hearts of everyone you have touched and nurtured while you were here."

That philosophy provided much solace as my wife, two children, and I had to cope with the loss of our friend, advisor, and confidant, Fr. John Savoca, parochial vicar of St. James the Apostle, who left this world on November 29, 1999. Fr. John's non-traditional path to the priesthood gave him a unique insight and a perspective that so effectively helped him bridge the gap between the secular and spiritual realms.

A father and grandfather, Fr. John entered the priesthood after being widowed. The love and pride he had for his family was endlessly evident to all around him. This greatly enhanced his spirituality and drew him closer to those of us who made him part of our families. During the mid-1980s, as an employee of the Archdiocese of New York, I met somewhere in the vicinity of 400 parish priests. As in any field, those who enter the religious life represent a wide spectrum of backgrounds and personalities. None, however, in my experience, conveyed the essence of God as did Fr. John.

One of the most enjoyable evenings of my life was spent with Fr. John, sitting at the table of the St. James rectory kitchen.

We began by discussing a topic for which I was interviewing him for an article I was working on, but as is wont to happen, we moved on to other topics like life, families, religion, the church, and a myriad of others, important and trivial, that served to display the wisdom, faith, and love of a remarkable man.

There are so many little memories and reminders of his visits to our home. Items blessed for us and as gifts for others, each blessing personalized and unique. The little red toy Porsche that sits on the base of my son Justin's bed table lamp. The baptism card, with a personal poem by Fr. John, given to my daughter Marygrace. The words of compassion and strength given to my wife Marie on the death of our beloved twenty-three year old Calico cat, as Fr. John shared the pain he still felt over the loss of his own cat years earlier. The joy of finding him waiting for us before mass at Our Lady of the Lake a year earlier to ask that we light the first Advent candle as a family.

It will be painful not seeing Fr. John's smiling face, hearing his voice, and receiving his wisdom from the pulpit and at home. That one last phone call we had and the visit he shared with Marie and the children in his final days will be cherished. Although in his illness he optimistically hoped to be able to come to our house for another dinner, one including Marie's "red sauce" which he so looked forward to, it was not to be.

Still, perhaps we will sit down one day soon, to a meal of what Fr. John would have so enjoyed. After all, as Morrie Schwartz reminded us all, "Death ends a life, not a relationship."

"Old Friend Knew Value of the Past"

"You are almost the only one left that I can still reminisce about the old times with," long time family friend and Putnam County Historian Dick Muscarella said that to my father when they spent time together one November. My parents had come home to New York for a visit a year after having retired to Florida.

Reminisce they did. They recalled the hunting trips and

local politics. They remembered their gun club buddies in the fading photographs. Old friends from the days when hometown meant everyone knew everyone else. Old friends from a time when mailmen and cops walked their beats. When there was only one grocery store in town and the women at the cash registers knew everyone's name. Friends from a time when gas station attendants cleaned your windshield and checked your oil, and doctors made house calls. Old friends wondering where the years had gone and wondering too when they turned from parents into grandparents, from young upstarts to town elders.

When Dick passed away two months later, a large part of the county's living history went with him. He had farmed the land before I was born. Before condominiums and before many of the paved roads we now drive on even existed. Over the years he put up drywall in many of the homes we live in, and he shared his love of history with many of us as a substitute teacher in the high school. He saw our county change from a rural farming community to the growing suburb it continues to be.

His death took friends and family by surprise in spite of the health issues he had been battling. He rarely, if ever, missed a day in his office as county historian. A mutual friend commented to me that he had spent time in Dick's office just days before his death and observed his familiar passion and vitality. His dedication to preserving the past was still being discharged with the same devotion and perhaps a hint of urgency.

My feeling of loss, I realize, came not just from all the years when he had been a family friend, but also from the fact that we were kindred spirits of a sort. Through his work preserving the county's history, he gave the past a value, a significance, and a sense of reverence that many ignore or take for granted. The historical markers he made sure were in place for all to see. The ancient ledgers he saw preserved so future generations will know how their ancestors shaped the world they live in. All of the things that say, "The little things that make up the past are actually the big things that make up our lives."

Through my work as a journalist and poet, I constantly feel the draw of the past. The ordinary people who turn out to be extraordinary. The common places that hold all of the world's adventure. The simple times that in reality encompass all of life's complexities. Everything has roots in that which came before.

I first learned of Dick's passing when my father called me from Florida. News had traveled to him twelve hundred miles away before reaching me in the same town in which Dick lived. As one devoted to preserving the simpler times when neighbors knew everything about each other, I suspect that Dick would have enjoyed the irony of that.

~

Write about a time of great loss or serious illness. Hold nothing back.

Material Things

I have a five-disc CD changer in my living room and single disc models in my bedroom and den with all kinds of fancy programming capabilities. I also have an old brown Philco radio – AM only – that needs a new cord. The Philco has an orange glow when it plays in the dark which is where I used it the most growing up. The biggest hits of 1972 sounded especially good coming from it, and they have never sounded better even with all of the latest equipment and innovations.

Objects from our past can hold the keys to who we are and why we treasure and value certain things over others. That's why tag sales, flea markets, and online auctions are so popular. As writers we often over sentimentalize and cling to the past. That is a good thing. It helps us bring passion to our work. We can then help others to the realization that they can still relate to the little things that meant so much to them.

I used to listen to New York's WABC every night in bed and on the weekends sitting on my thick orange carpet, adjusting the tuning needle to just the right place to pull in 77 on the dial. My favorite disc jockey lineup still comes rushing back: Harry Harrison, Run Lundy, and Dan Ingram all day; Cousin Bruce Morrow, Chuck Leonard, and Jay Reynolds all night; and Frank Kingston Smith and Johnny Donovan on the weekends. For a number of years, as I graduated to stereo systems and moved out of my parents' house, I did not think about that old brown radio. Then one day it became an obsession to find it. I cannot recall what triggered the need, but it was as strong a desire as I have ever felt for a piece of nostalgia.

I rummaged around my parents' garage which was filled with car parts, rusty furniture, and dusty 78 rpm records. My heart sunk when I came across the caseless insides of a radio that looked to be the appropriate size and had the needle-sharp dial that looked about as I remembered it. It was balanced precariously on top of some sort of short wave receiver and a big old-fashioned box type radio that once broadcast things like *Fibber Magee and Molly*, *Gangbusters*, and *The Shadow*. I realized that my old brown radio must have been scavenged for parts as it lay neglected for so many years. Upon closer inspection however, I saw that the name "Philco" was nowhere to be found.

Grasping for straws, I pulled down the stairs to the attic and ascended although I certainly would have remembered having seen it there over the years if that was where it had ended up. There were stacks of board games like Candy Land, Masterpiece, and Concentration that had long been discarded. There were suitcases thick with dust, an American flag in its original box, and an Indian headdress, but no old brown radio.

As I turned to leave, my flashlight knocked over a souvenir monorail from the 1964 World's Fair. It landed on the plywood floor right beside the sought after symbol of my adolescence. I cleaned up my old brown radio and it looked wonderful. I have not yet gotten around to replacing the dried out cord that has kept me from trying to play it. Still, even if it never plays again, it sure feels good to have my old brown radio back.

***

When I was young, one of my favorite toys was a tin Midtown Service Station made by the Marx company. Today it would be made of plastic, especially the sign that hung from its side with its sharp edges. The cars, gas pumps, and other accessories were plastic and there was a red ramp inside that the cars rolled down from the rooftop parking area. There was an elevator that worked on a string when you turned a little crank. I used to play with it for hours on end. When I was older, the service station, along with my G.I. Joe, met its demise when my younger brother received a super 8 movie camera and decide to become a horror film producer. The gas station went up in flames, and Joe was blown up in the bloody climax of one of my brother's stop action "masterpieces." I have been able to replace G.I. Joe and my beloved Batman cards thanks to faithful reproductions and reissues in recent years. As for the Midtown Service Station, I will have to keep combing eBay until one appears that is not rusted beyond recognition.

~

Fill a box with mementos from your childhood. Write about what each meant to you and of the memories each brings back.

The Nine Dots

Whenever I begin teaching a writing workshop or a course with students of any age level, I start them off with an old brainteaser puzzle. It is the one with nine dots arranged in three even rows of three. The object of the puzzle is to connect the nine dots by using four straight lines, never picking up your pencil, and not backtracking over any lines. From elementary school to college and beyond, students grapple with the puzzle, ultimately deciding that there must be a trick to it. I tell them that, no, there is no trick. You just need to think like a writer.

The reason this simple little puzzle becomes so frustrating is that inevitably the students assume that the dots must be connected to look like a box since they are laid out in three rows that imply a square. The solution is to go outside of the matrix, and at that point "going outside the box" however cliché it might sound, becomes the catch phrase for our time together. Writers need to remove the limitations that they impose on themselves, to break down the walls.

Growing as a writer is like growing in any other way. Mostly it just sneaks up on you. You don't feel it happening, but one day your shoes don't fit anymore. One day you read something you wrote some time earlier and think, "That's not half bad."

Thinking like a writer is an acquired way of looking at the world. I always ask my students what their experience would be like going to a baseball game and focusing on left field for the entire nine innings rather than home plate and the pitcher's mound like everyone else. They would see a different game for sure, but it would provide the opportunity to write about that game from outside the box in which all the other spectators would be trapped. They would see things everyone else missed. One of the pieces of advice offered most often to aspiring journalists is "find the gravedigger" a reference to an interview conducted by the young Jimmy Breslin who when covering the Kennedy assassination in 1963, used as a vantage point the man whose job it was to dig the grave for the slain president.

I went to a gymnastics exhibition featuring the seven members of the United States Women's Olympic Team shortly after they won the gold medal at the 1996 summer games in Atlanta. The crowd was clearly enamored with Shannon Miller, Dominique Moceanu, Kerri Strug, and the rest of the "magnificent seven" and was watching their every move.

I did not focus my attention on one of the seven, but rather on Kim Zmeskal, who at the 1992 games was justifiably considered the nation's best hope for gold, but whose fall from the balance beam squelched that dream. Now, she was no longer the petite, serious-eyed teenager, America's sweetheart, but a mature woman of twenty: smiling, graceful, and muscular.

As I watched her, I was not seeing the media frenzy surrounding the Atlanta team, but the fruits of dedication, commitment, and courage – coming back from injury to triumph as much if not more than the others.

This time, as she stepped on the beam, the music was poignant and perfect. Madonna's "This Used to be My Playground" accompanied Kim Zmeskal's flawless performance with lyrics talking of looking back with no regrets. It was a moment perhaps lost on others caught up in the hype enveloping the Olympic team, but to me it was the highlight of the show.

I was working with Kevin, a high school student, on an art history independent study project. We spent two days in New York City visiting museums. He took pages and pages of notes for the essays he was to write. I was there as a tutor with no personal agenda in mind.

As we viewed paintings, both modern and classic, artifacts, sculptures, and photographs, I found myself jotting down notes on the admission tickets and exhibition flyers. While the works of art were inspiring, I was now seeing them differently from the way I had viewed them in the past. I saw them through the eyes of others in the museum. This experience became a poem called "Looking at Girls Looking at Art."

The point is that there are two levels to writing. Competent writing is relatively easy to achieve. You check spelling, sentence structure, topic sentences, paragraph development, and consult a grammar handbook. That other level is trickier but far more essential. You need to make your writing unique and specific and raise the sophistication level. Look at the girls looking at art. Watch the left fielder. Look to the side of the spotlight. Find the gravedigger. Tear down the walls and go outside the box.

"Ends of a Spectrum"

I found it interesting one semester that among the students in a college composition course I was teaching, the two students who consistently produced the highest quality work were the oldest and youngest in the group. Frank had returned to college after many years and could have been the parent of his classmates. He had graying hair and sported a hearing aid. Gwen had a ponytail, braces, and was at twelve years old, a high school graduate, and a college freshman.

Why were these two "nontraditional" students from opposite ends of a spectrum the top students in the class? I asked Frank what he thought. "Perhaps the similarities that Gwen and I share are those usually reserved for the very young. The freedom to try new things and the excitement that follows, and most important of all, no fear of failure. I think we lose those things as we attain adulthood, and maybe, as in my case, get them back at a later date. I remember someone saying that we start out in life with no teeth, eating crackers and warm milk, and we wind up our lives the same way."

They both had something else. Each was able to approach the class from a different perspective, from outside the box.

~

Write about an event from a perspective that does not seem to be the most obvious vantage point.

Preserving Special Moments

Sometimes there is just the desire to write something down. It may never go anywhere beyond your journal, but it will not stop spinning around in your mind until you get it down on paper for fear of losing the feelings attached to it. Other times it is just a moment that you know may never come again. I recall the great poet Kenneth Koch telling a story in a class in which I was a student. He had gone to a reading by Marianne Moore, the famous poet, and had brought along one of her books for her to sign. She told him she would sign it but it would have to be a gift to him from her. With that, the elderly Moore pulled out a tiny change purse and began counting out the price of the book. After more than a little haggling, he was able to dissuade her from that, but she then asked him if he would walk her home. He agreed and when they got to her apartment building she said, "Now you must have your reward." He feared that she was about to the pull out the change purse again, but instead she pointed to a droopy, floppy-eared dog lying on the sidewalk and said, "There is your reward." One great poet pointing out to another a momentary bit of inspiration from the ordinariness of life.

There was magic in the air on the night of my twenty-year high school reunion in 1998. Unlike our previous get together ten years earlier, there was no sense of anyone trying to impress anyone else. We actually felt like "grown ups" after all those years. It was filled with little moments and personal epiphanies. It was late by the time I got home, too late to logically start anything except the pre-sleep rituals, but so many different ideas and memories were flowing through my head, I had to get them down. It was a long, occasionally rambling, thirty-five hundred words in stream of consciousness that eventually I edited to a five hundred or so word newspaper column. The original, banged out in the wee hours of a summer morning, remains special to me. It is not polished. It does not flow particularly well and it would be of little interest to another reader.

There have been other times that I have allowed my pen

to move quickly along the pages of a notebook to capture a moment I did not want to lose. Sometimes we just write for ourselves because it is a nice thing to do. These personal journal excerpts do not necessarily rank among my "best" or most marketable writings, but they are pieces that I enjoy revisiting from time to time.

April 28, 2003.

Jane Elliott, the teacher who did the brown eyes/blue eyes experiment known as *The Eye of the Storm,* gave a lecture at the college where I teach. The experiment was designed to teach children about prejudice in the wake of the Martin Luther King assassination, and I had seen the television documentary about it in around 1970 when I was an elementary school student. I had to teach a class the night of the lecture so could not attend, but I waited outside the theater in the student center for her to arrive. Members of the university's centennial committee, which had arranged for the visit, escorted her into the building. A woman with her seemed to recognize me as a staff member and asked if I was coming to the lecture. I said I had to get to a class, but hoped to have a chance to at least meet Mrs. Elliott. She introduced us and we had a chance to talk. I told her how I had seen *The Eye of the Storm* when I was nine or ten and how it made an impact on me and was part of what made me want to teach. I told her that seeing the impact one person could have as a teacher inspired me to enter the profession. She was moved and said, "Thank you for becoming a teacher." I told her it was a pleasure and that although I had to get to a class, I just could not pass up an opportunity to meet her. She was happy to sign the flyer I had with me that had her picture on it and was used on campus to publicize her appearance. I realized that she was a teaching hero.

November 10, 2003.

I did a full day of readings and workshops at a school and then a college poetry workshop. I ended the workshop early, asking the students to follow me to a nearby Borders bookstore where writer Mike Lupica was doing a discussion and book signing. He did a humorous talk about sports and his books. During questions, I told him that his columns outside of the sports pages on which he usually appears contained some of my favorite examples of his work and asked how he would feel if he were asked to leave sports and write full-time for the op-ed pages. He thanked me for mentioning some of the specific columns and added that as long as he has access to the front of the paper whenever he wants to write for it, he likes staying in sports because it is different every day and "if it was good enough for Red Smith" it was good enough for him. He talked of how legendary sports writer Dick Young never liked him and was miserable toward him when he arrived in New York as a kid reporter. He explained that he got the bug to write in high school and saw a photo of Jimmy Breslin at an old manual typewriter and knew that was for him. "If the writing ever dries up," he said, "I have no other skills." I bought a copy of his new book *Red Zone* and had it signed for me, and a copy of *Summer of '98*, his brilliant book about baseball and the father-son legacy it represents, I had him sign for my son Justin. When I told him it was for my son, for whom I leave notes in the morning after games that are on too late for him to stay up to watch (like Mike wrote of doing for his sons), he mentioned how he had been talking to his father about that same thing earlier in the day.

Friday, October 1, 2004.

I received a phone call tonight from Pamela Leonard, the widow of Chuck Leonard, who was one of my favorite disc jockeys and one of those who had inspired my ten year career in the field. Chuck passed away about a month ago and when she was going through some things she found, among some records, an unopened envelope that I had sent to him in 1998 at the radio station where he was then working. It contained a photo of the air staff of WABC in the 1960s that four of the other disc jockeys with whom Chuck had worked had signed. I had sent it with the hope of adding his signature to the others. She went through the trouble of finding my phone number because she assumed the photo was important to me, and she wanted to be sure that the self-addressed stamped envelope that I had included with a note asking Chuck to add his signature to the photo still contained a current address. We had a nice talk about her late husband and of the impact of his death. It was a very classy thing of her to do.

~

Write about a time when an ordinary day became memorable because of someone you met or because of something nice someone did for you.

Perseverance Pays Off

At the time, I did not know how important they would be to me a quarter of a century later, but when I was in adolescence some of my best friends were the faceless voices drifting out of my transistor radio. From "Brandy (You're a Fine Girl)" to "Crocodile Rock," from "American Pie" to "Beach Baby" the songs I loved can still take me back to those times of self-doubt and confusion, to carefree summer days and endless summer nights. There were days of being too sick to go to school, but never too sick to wait expectantly for the week's top hit to play one more time. The only sound with a stronger power than the songs to transport me back to those shadows of yesterday are the voices of the disc jockeys who brought them to me. Eventually I decided to assemble what has become the most treasured part of my autograph collection: signed photos of the radio personalities I grew up with. The WABC New York on-air staff of the early '70s was my favorite. Fortunately, most of the eight jocks were still in the Big Apple more than twenty years later when I began my quest and were most generous in responding to my requests.

Harry Harrison, Dan Ingram, Ron Lundy, and Bruce "Cousin Brucie" Morrow were still broadcasting over oldies station WCBS-FM. Chuck Leonard was with urban formatted WBLS, and Johnny Donovan had stayed on as production manager when WABC became a talk station in 1982. I had long ago lost track of overnight host Jay Reynolds, ultimately learning (when he passed away in 1996) that he had returned to Indianapolis after leaving New York in 1976.

Still missing from my collection was Frank Kingston Smith, one of the DJs who gave me some of my best memories. He was on the air Saturday nights and Sunday afternoons with humor and warmth and was one of the voices that inspired me to work in the industry. Maybe it was his seemingly effortless delivery or maybe just the genuine fun he seemed to be having, but in any case, I was hooked on Top 40 radio for life. Even though he was in New York for a shorter time than the others on the staff, he was there for the years that rock and roll radio had the biggest impact on me and served as the musical score of my life.

My first attempt to contact him was through the announcers' union. I sent a letter along with several articles I had published about the heyday of Top 40 radio. Much time went by with no response. I recalled that he had left New York to work in Boston radio and did a bit of research to find out what station he had been with most recently. One person I spoke with at a station in Boston said, "Frank? Yeah, I think he's in Arizona somewhere." A search during the relatively early days of the Internet turned up an e-mail address for a Frank Kingston Smith, but he did not turn out to be the one I was seeking.

I was disappointed in not being able to contact him, but not just because I could not obtain an autograph. I wanted to tell him how much his broadcasts had meant to me. Grasping at straws, I put together another package of my articles and another letter explaining the situation and apologizing if it was the second time he was receiving the same mailing from me. Once again I sent it in care of the union.

Much to my delight, about a week later I received a large envelope return addressed from F.K.Smith in Arizona. It contained two WABC mementos that I had sent asking him to sign, along with a recent signed photo, "Just so you can see I am aging gracefully," he wrote in a thoughtful letter. The letter explained that since leaving radio in 1993, he had continued doing voice-over and movie work, and that he also produces and announces flying shows around the country and internationally.

He added that my first letter never got to him and said, "I miss the 'old' WABC and NYC. I had a great time there. Fine people and wonderful memories." I was glad I had not given up and that eventually I found that someone I admire is as kind and thoughtful as I had hoped. Perseverance paid off in this case, and can do so in a writing career as well.

Turndown letters and unopened submissions are an integral part of a writer's life. They come in batches early on, then if you stick with it, with less frequency, and eventually even with encouraging little notes scrawled on the bottom. One fact remains through a writer's career – they will come.

One of the articles that I sent to Frank was about Musicradio 77, WABC New York, the most successful Top 40 station ever. It was an integral part of my life as a kid growing up in suburbia and was an article I felt I was born to write. Bringing it to the printed page provided a lesson about perseverance that has since served me well.

During a phone conversation with an editor at *Discoveries*, a magazine devoted to records and CDs, I pitched the idea, figuring an article about a radio station that used to help break the hits would be a logical tie-in. He expressed enough of an interest for me to get going. I contacted and interviewed either by phone or through the mail Harry Harrison, Dan Ingram, Bruce Morrow, Ed Baer, and Joe O'Brien, all of whom had either worked at WABC or for its main competitor WMCA. I painstakingly transcribed the interviews, organized the quotes, and wrote and rewrote a narrative tracing the golden age of Rock and Roll radio from Alan Freed through the Beatles era to the fall of AM rock. I packaged the manuscript titled "Amplitude Modulations – The Rise and Fall of AM Rock and Roll Radio" with related photos and the required self-addressed stamped envelope and sent it on its way.

Weeks went by and then came the letter that I had never anticipated. It was complimentary but indicated that the piece was not related closely enough to the record industry to be of interest to the publication's readers.

A bit of time went by and almost as a second thought I pitched the idea to the editor of a glossy nostalgia magazine called *Remember*. He said he had fond memories of the time period and personalities I was talking about and that if the piece had a least something of a national focus he would be interested. I quickly added a few references to radio stations and disc jockeys from markets outside of New York, which remained the main focus of the piece. It was accepted immediately for the highest payment I had received for an article to that date.

When the issue with the article came out, I was very happy with the layout and presentation, and it was well received. I realized that I still had lots of great material that had not appeared in the piece and continued to indulge my passion for radio. I was a regular contributor to *Autograph Times,* so I added a storyline about the intimate connection disc jockeys have with their audiences and packaged it with some 8 x 10 autographed photos of my favorite disc jockeys. I submitted it and had another radio byline, a cover story titled "Stacks of Wax: Collecting DJ Autographs."

Next I banged out a review of one of my references, Wolfman Jack's autobiography *Have Mercy: Confessions of the Original Rock 'n' Roll Animal* and placed it in *English Journal's* Bedside Table column. That made three bylines stemming from a turndown letter.

As any of us who have worked in radio know, radio people love to talk about radio. When I interviewed Bruce Morrow, everything he said was a story, everything quotable. The county was in a new wave of Beatlemania with the release of the group's *Anthology* documentary and CDs. His recollections of covering the Beatles during the British Invasion of the sixties became "Crusin' with Cousin Brucie and the Beatles" which appeared in *Yesterday's Magazette.* Byline number four.

A recurring theme in my research was how talk radio replaced music on the AM band and became a new pop cultural phenomenon. That became my fifth radio story, another *Autograph Times* cover piece titled "Icons of Talk Radio." The focus was not all that different from the disc jockey story and suggested that the talk radio hosts would become the fondly remembered voices for today's generation.

My sixth rejection-inspired byline would appear in *The Putnam Courier-Trader.* The focus became being nostalgic for the simple days of growing up in the suburbs listening to the "All Americans" and the "Good Guys" on a transistor radio. A few local references were added to slant the piece to the region served by the newspaper.

An issue of *English Journal* had a call for manuscripts dealing with media literacy. As an English teacher, I had already begun incorporating my interest in radio into my classroom and put together an article titled "Radio: The Intimate Medium" discussing assignments, lessons, and projects that can be built around radio. A personal essay then appeared in *The Nimham Times Magazine*, a regional publication, in which I reflected on my years as a local radio personality. That made eight bylines born of one rejection.

If you have faith in a piece, stick with it. Develop new angles and expand existing ones. Find ways to make local ideas global and global ideas local. Become a recycler.

***

When I was writing the sequence of poems that became my chapbook *Summer Rising, River Flowing*, I had a great deal of trouble making it work. I had about two-dozen poems but could not come up with a "voice" or "perspective" or tense that served to pull it together as a unified entity. I struggled mightily and was even resigned to the thought that maybe it just would never come together. I turned to poems and poets that over the years had provided me with inspiration, but again, nothing worked. Finally, I remembered *Spoon River Anthology* by Edgar Lee Masters, where different voices spoke from a cemetery. I decided to use as many points of view as necessary, one for each poem if need be, and to return to my collection. Once I did that, something very exciting began to happen. It was as if the poems were writing themselves from the voices of the fictional, and occasionally the real, people who might have experienced the onset, destruction, and aftermath of Hurricane Agnes in 1972.

~

Pick a story, article, or poem you have worked on (or would like to write.) Create a draft you are happy with. Submit and revise it until you find a home for it.

When Life Gets in the Way

I suppose anyone who is a writer or dreams of being one, has imagined living the stereotypical writer's life. Owning few possessions and having very little cash. Nobody to answer to except a leather bound journal, earning enough to pay the rent on a small Greenwich Village studio through the occasional seminar or artist in residence week, maybe living in a cabin in the woods with a little lake to bathe in as the sun comes up.

I don't have that writer's life. I have a wife, a son, a daughter, a mortgage, car payments, and a second mortgage. I have a full-time job teaching middle school English, an adjunct position teaching college writing, and commitments to a number of students whom I tutor. Possessions? I have more books, videotapes, and CDs than I will ever have shelf space for.

Writers talk of writing as being a way of life. How can you make writing a way of life when the responsibilities and distractions of everyday life seem to be your way of life? There are ways to do it. Start by keeping things in perspective. I feel very fortunate to have work that I enjoy that allows me to pay the bills. Does that cut into my writing time? Perhaps. Or maybe my time needs to be redistributed somehow. When I get into a routine, even if it is only for thirty or forty-five minutes a day, writing becomes as natural as showering, reading the newspaper, or driving to work. I don't need to think about when or how or even how well I do these things. I just do them. The writing becomes easier and better too.

Find out what works for you. One summer I found that getting up early in the morning before everyone else and writing from 5:30 to 7:30 worked well. At other times, staying up until two and working after everyone else had gone to bed served me well. There was a stretch when one of my children was just born when writing in the morning after the four o'clock feeding was a tremendously fertile time.

How do you write when it seems there is a distraction at every turn? Start by turning off the television. It is amazing how much more productive that will make you. Take care of the interruptions before they occur. Before I disappear into the basement for a writing session, I try to take care of as much of my "to do" list as possible. Is the garbage emptied, is there laundry that needs to be carried upstairs, are there phone calls that need to be made? After that, I don't have things on my mind that I still need to do, just some uninterrupted writing time.

When the interruptions occur anyway, which sometimes they will, do not waste time overreacting and explaining how the interruption affects your work. It is much more expedient to take the phone call, change the baby, or watch the stove for a minute. Learn to ignore the mess in your workspace. It should have little to do with what goes on in your head. I have windows in front of my desk and books to the sides. If I face the window, I don't even see the piles of outgrown clothes, boxes of no longer used toys, crates of holiday decorations, and someday-to-be-antique furniture behind me.

If during your day you can find a private, almost secret, place to write for a while, do so. It will give you the feeling of doing something special even if it is just for the time it takes to finish a cup of coffee and return to your non-writing work.

Above all else be prepared and keep writing. Be sure to have pens and paper everywhere – in the car, in your pockets, next to your bed – so as not to lose any idea that might flit by. Some of my best work has stemmed from fragments scribbled on the morning newspaper while driving to work.

As I look back at an ever increasing body of work, I realize that so many of my favorite and most successful pieces have been written about the very things that seemed to stand in the way of living "the writer's life." The joys and occasional hazards of raising children. The trials and occasional triumphs of teaching. Personal and professional obligations that cut into the hours of a day and break life's routine. Strangely enough, I have come to feel that given the wherewithal to live the stereotypical writer's life, I would be lacking the very things that provide something to write about.

The traditional writer's life – the simple, reclusive,

Bohemian life – might just be best left alongside Walden Pond. As for me, I'll take the one with the hectic schedules, the chronic interruptions, and the mortgage and electric bills every month. It gives me something to write about.

***

    The 2004 Fall semester started and with it came the full days of teaching, the college courses taught at night, tutoring here and there in the afternoons, and all of the other things that prove that there are not enough hours in the day. I decided to dedicate my lunch period, 12:15-12:57, each day to working on this book. It became one of the most productive stretches of writing that I have ever experienced. It also helped me become more efficient with other things. I so looked forward to that writing time, that I was sure to take care of any other responsibilities that might get in the way.

    ~

    Write for at least twenty minutes a day for at least two weeks. Get up earlier or stay up later. Cut lunch short. Get to work early.

The Wonder Years

Let's face it. We all knew deep down that we would never reside in those two bedrooms with the adjoining bathroom with the six Brady kids. We knew too that we would never really ride the bus with Keith, Danny, Laurie, and the rest of the Partridges. But Kevin Arnold and Winnie Cooper, they were different. Anyone who grew up in the late 60s and early 70s was Kevin, or Winnie, or at least Paul, Becky, Carla or one of the other friends or siblings who appeared in the 115 episodes of *The Wonder Years*. The names might have been changed to protect the innocent, but the experiences from first love to first car, were extracted from our own lives.

During its run from 1988 to 1993, the series not only preserved the emotions, joys, and pains of growing up in a tumultuous era, but also showed that movies, television, books, and music profoundly affected who we were and how we thought. By using our popular culture, the series was even more effective in preserving our youth and allowing us to experience it one more time.

My wonder years included a main street that had everything a kid with a pocketful of loose change could want. Kurtz's for candy and comic books, Fogel's five and dime for sling shots and Matchbox cars, and soda fountains at both Cornish's and Simpson's drug stores. A couple of more years and a slightly longer walk led to 45 rpm records for sixty-nine cents at Barkers and thirty-five cent slices of pizza on waxed paper at Segretti's. Those carefree days would culminate with double features at the Mahopac Drive-In.

One of the best things about being a teacher is having the same schedule that I grew up with. A fresh start each September, Christmas break, snow days, the countdown in June. In many ways, it is like getting a chance to relive the simplicities, difficulties, and heartbreaks of growing up all over again. There are no longer drive-in movie theaters playing double features into the wee hours of the morning and pizza is rarely served on those little sheets of waxed paper, but young people still fall in love, worry about tests, and think sports are far more important than world affairs. Maybe they are right.

When *The Wonder Years* premiered, I was among an entire generation that was allowed to relive the memories of growing up. Like any collection of memories, the series was episodic with some underlying strings of continuity. Through Kevin Arnold, the protagonist of the series, it was possible to vicariously relive all of those precious, prized, and painful moments that make up adolescence. From first kiss, to the breakup of the love that was to last forever, from the first job to growing up and letting go, the challenges, achievements, disappointments, and successes of Kevin Arnold were shared by us all.

When the inevitable announcement came that the series was cancelled in 1993, I felt cheated, for *The Wonder Years* was ending its run a year short of Kevin, girlfriend Winnie, and best friend Paul becoming seniors in high school, a traditional rite of passage into adulthood. I was grateful for having had the opportunity to relive those special moments while at the same time had the feeling that my own adolescence had somehow ended for a second time.

Since honesty and realism were the hallmark of the series, perhaps it was the most appropriate ending of all that the series, like youth itself, faded to black just a little too soon.

"A Summer Thirty Years Ago"

"When I look back now, that summer seemed to last forever, and if I had the choice I'd always want to be there…those were the best days of my life…back in the summer of '69." It is hard to believe that those lyrics to the Bryan Adams hit from a few years back refer to a summer that has been gone for three decades now.

As I turned nine that Putnam County summer, I had, like most young Americans, a sort of cultural innocence that would soon turn to cynicism and doubt with the deepening of years, the resignation of a president in disgrace, and a widening global oil crisis. Still, before the '60s (an era of change and turbulence everywhere from college campuses to the popular music charts) gave way to the '70s, there was that one last summer: that summer of '69. We would walk "up street" to buy penny candy. The high school and post office looked huge even at half their present sizes. All of us neighborhood kids could play in our yards and catch pollywogs after dark, never worrying about our photos ending up on a flyer tacked to the grocery store wall.

It was a summer of sports upon which to build a lifetime of memories. Gil Hodges was leading the Miracle Mets into baseball history with Seaver, Koosman, Harrelson, Agee, Swoboda, and McGraw. Willis Reed, Walt "Clyde" Frazier, Dave DeBusschere, and the rest of the Knicks were among the favorites to compete for the NBA crown after Bill Russell's retirement from the Celtics. Fresh off his Super Bowl MVP performance, Joe Namath prepared to help the Jets try to defend their AFL title.

On Broadway, James Earl Jones was starring in *The Great White Hope*. Jackie Gleason was still on television on Saturday nights, while Sunday still meant *Bonanza* and *Rowan and Martin's Laugh-in* was redefining comedy on Mondays. *Easy Rider* cruised into movie theaters. The top spot on the pop music charts was occupied that summer by the Beatles' "Get Back," Henry Mancini's "Love Theme from Romeo and Juliet," "In the Year 2525" by the never again heard from duo Zager and Evans, and the Rolling Stones' "Honky Tonk Woman."

July 20 came that summer, and with it the culmination of a challenge set forth at the dawn of the decade by President Kennedy. From the countdown and launch, to the splash down and capsule recovery in the ocean, each flight of the Apollo program was a adventure to us kids. That July evening in '69 when Neil Armstrong took the first steps on the lunar surface, man's limitations seemed to disappear.

Less than a month later, at a farm in a small upstate town, Joan Baez, Richie Havens, Jimi Hendrix, Country Joe and the Fish, Melanie, and a long list of others gathered to perform at the generation-defining Woodstock Music and Arts Festival.

Today, a generation raised on *Star Wars* and Power

Rangers finds the space program a bit old hat. Indeed, my seventh graders were largely unimpressed when we provided school-wide television access to John Glenn's return to space. They know Woodstock as Snoopy's little yellow friend rather than an event that forever etched Bethel, NY into American pop culture.

Sad? Maybe. On the other hand you cannot create defining moments. We likely were unaware of the magnitude of the history being written during that endless summer of '69. What will be the defining moments for nine-year-olds this summer of '99? Hard to say, but certainly they will look back from the summer of 2029 with the same sense of awe and melancholy that the summer of '69 provides.

~

Write about the ways popular culture has affected and/or reflected your life. Think about literature, movies, music, theater, television, and sports. What do you miss about days gone by? What do you think will be timeless for you?

Low Tech in a High Tech World

I have never been particularly quick to give up old technology for the new. It was years before I would switch from my beloved vinyl records to compact discs. To this day I feel a twinge of longing when I have to read CD liner notes with a magnifying glass. When the classic sports networks replay old baseball games with almost no on-screen graphics, I am reminded of why I prefer baseball on the radio over the cablecasts with cameras capturing the action from every angle including the catcher's mask.

By the time my daughter Marygrace was five she could manipulate a mouse with more dexterity than anyone I know. She was using words like "CD-Rom" and "download" the way my generation used "pencil" and "pen." I readily admit to being low tech. I am drafting the words you are reading by hand on a yellow legal pad. Eventually I will put them on a disc and make revisions. As technology becomes more and more a part of our lives, we need to remain aware that content and the human creative process are still more important than presentation. As writers, we need to pass on the knowledge that clip art, scanned photos, and fancy covers mean nothing without carefully crafted words.

To what extent you embrace technology is of course an individual decision. Early in my writing career I realized that the time had come to invest in a home computer with Internet access when the editor of a major New York City newspaper and I agreed on a freelance assignment. She needed the copy fairly quickly and asked, "Can you get it to me on a floppy disc?"

"Um, I'm not sure if my personal word processor will put it in a format you will be able to convert."

"That's all right; you can just fax it to me."

"Yeah, I can get to a fax machine somewhere."

Finally she paused for a moment and said, "Let me just give you my Fed Ex account number and you can send it that way. You sure are low tech aren't you?"

I knew it was time to find a middle ground on this technology stuff or risk becoming the Greg Kinnear character in *You've Got Mail* – a columnist in love with his manual typewriter. I learned to send manuscripts electronically, and I have to admit that it is a fun challenge to have an editor ask that some final revisions be submitted within twenty minutes of when the newspaper goes to bed. While high speed searches and easy access to volumes of information have made life easier in many situations, and I use the Internet as regularly as a telephone, radio, or television, I still miss the days of searching the dusty stacks of a library for a source that might not have been signed out for several decades.

Use technology to your benefit and do not be intimidated by it. Cars replaced horse and carriage and life went on. The electric light replaced candles and life went on. The microwave replaced reheating on the stovetop and life went on.

As much as technology has improved life and has made it easier in a multitude of ways, there is one area in which I will never be convinced that high tech is an improvement. Nothing will ever match the feeling of receiving a hand-written letter from a friend – one that has been folded, placed in an envelope addressed to me, licked with a loved one's tongue, sealed with the same loved one's fingers, stamped, and placed in a mailbox to be delivered to me by human hands.

I have more to say on this topic, but right now I have to go and check my e-mail.

"A Perfect Day"

When I stop and take a breath and step out of the fast paced day-to-day existence we call life, I realize how important it is to remember the simple things that make up that which really matters. It is the end of a day near the end of a summer early in the twenty-first century. I feel the long humid days of summer melt into the cooler, shorter days of fall. I look back at the things that made this summer another special one: watching the fireworks over Lake Carmel with my wife and children, seeing the joy on their faces as Justin and Marygrace catch fireflies in the backyard of their godparents, taking my son to his first game at Yankee Stadium, in spite of the 12-2 loss. I imagine for a moment a day when all of those good things blend with past times and people, some with us, some long gone, to form one day. One perfect day…

Joe and Pauline Greene are still selling the morning newspapers and George's Place still finds George behind the counter. Father John Savoca celebrates morning Mass at St. James and Michael's hot dog truck is still parked by the Putnam Plaza.

The Yankees lead the Red Sox by half a game in the American League East with Boston in town for a showdown at the stadium. Catfish Hunter is on the mound with Thurman Munson behind the plate. There is a new episode of *The Wonder Years* on tonight and one of *The Honeymooners* too.

Tiny, the black and white terrier, barks and runs in circles as she detects the brakes of my grandparents' 1953 Packard a block away. Jim Croce has a new album in release and Harry Chapin is appearing in the Central Park Concert Series at the skating rink.

At midday the great Ron Lundy says, "Hello Luv," on WABC, while up the dial William B. Williams says, "Hello World," over WNEW. Jack Spector is on WMCA and Wolfman Jack still howls on WNBC until midnight.

Sue Truran, Marylou Westerholm, Jerry Mergardt, and Janet Canniff are still enlightening generations in the English annex at Carmel High. Jack Lemmon is in a new film at the Carmel Theater, Sean Connery plays James Bond at the Brewster Cameo, and a Disney double bill is at the Mahopac Drive-in. Sophie Ryder is walking up Fair Street. Adam Wagner is walking down, and kids can walk up or down at any time without fear.

Grandma Eva is having tea and matzo at bedtime. Aunt Mary is in her New Rochelle kitchen frying peppers that we will eat together while watching *All My Children*, Ceil and Albert are watching a sandlot game from the window of their Co-op City high-rise. Brian and I take the train to Grand Central and get half price theater tickets at Duffy Square. Jim, Bill, Rob, and I go to the Windmill Diner in Jim's VW Beetle to get cheeseburgers and Cokes.

Johnny Carson is still hosting *The Tonight Show*. The night sky is clear with the constellations in full view. Marie and I look to the heavens as Justin and Marygrace sleep inside.

~

Look around your house. Make a list of all of the technological innovations introduced during your lifetime. How has each made life easier or harder? Write about how your life would change if they were removed from your life.

Set Your Writing Free

Great satisfaction can be derived from writing for yourself. Journals let you revisit times that might otherwise be lost. Ultimately, though, writers seek a wider audience. That takes courage and faith. The courage to put your writing out into the world to see what happens, and the faith that no matter what happens, your writing is, was, and will remain a part of who you are.

Singer-songwriter Tom Chapin once told me that in his estimation two of his songs "Family Tree" and "This Pretty Planet" have the best chance to "live on." The latter in particular has taken on a life of its own having been performed by Chapin's inspiration, folk legend Pete Seeger as well as being beamed to the astronauts on the John Glenn Shuttle flight. The song also reached a national audience on the ABC television newsmagazine *20/20* in a segment about paralyzed actor Christopher Reeve. Once you take the step of putting your work out there, you never know where it might take you. I once did an Internet search and came across an article that I had written in the works cited list of a research paper that someone had posted online. Another time I was driving to work in the morning listening to disc jockey Harry Harrison on WCBS-FM. Suddenly, he began talking about the interview we had done by telephone the night before.

In the spring and summer of 2003 when I had a couple of chapbooks in release and then following year when my book *Composite Sketches* came out, I scheduled a series of bookstore signings, gallery readings, and open mic appearances. Some were well attended, others had just a few friends there in support. Some were at chain stores like Barnes & Noble and Borders while others were at some of the wonderful independent bookstores that have managed to survive among the superstores and on-line booksellers. As I did the public readings, I surprised myself.

I have always been more than willing to turn down a public speaking opportunity if given the choice. I made a conscious decision that it was an important part of the writing process to personally put my words out into the world. This is what motivated me to set up the readings in the first place. Additionally, I learned long ago that if you do not promote yourself and your work, nobody else is likely to do it for you. I found that not only did I enjoy doing the readings and deciding which poems to use and in which order and what stories to tell, but also that I had a new perspective on my own work. Some poems work better on paper, others work better being performed.

The bottom line is to get your work out there. Share things you are working on in whatever venues are available to you. Don't be afraid to share your material that has not been "published" by someone else. What is publishing if not putting words on paper and having others read them? When you have "clips" (published pieces) make copies and send them to people you know (and some you do not know) who might have an interest in them. You never know where your words might end up and what responses might come back to you.

***

The first "fan" letter I ever received was from a teacher in Alameda, California. He came across a poem of mine that *English Journal* had published. In a complimentary letter, he referred to a couple of lines of the poem and said, "Funny, sometimes, how it takes someone else to help us find the sketch of what's really true." It was such a validating feeling and a testament to the power of the written word to have connected with a stranger three thousand miles away. After a newspaper column which I wrote following the death of a former teacher, whom I greatly admired, I received a note from his daughter, coincidentally from California as well, which said in part, "I was touched – in fact I cried...To know he had such an effect on you is a pleasure."

***

I have always made it a point to send copies of my finished articles to the people I have interviewed or who are mentioned. Here are a few random excerpts from notes that I have received in return that make for nice "bulletin board" affirmations when I need a reminder that I can put together words that matter.

"Thanks for the very accurate interview!" – Folk legend Pete Seeger.

"Thanks for the articles. You did a super job and I enjoyed reading them."– Long time New York morning disc jockey Harry Harrison.

"Thank you so much for sending your chapter on *In Country* (which appeared in the book *Rationales for Teaching Young Adult Literature*). I'm so grateful to teachers like you for keeping the book alive in the classroom."– Novelist Bobbie Ann Mason.

"Thank you for liking my work and for sending me your very interesting article." – Poet Kenneth Koch.

"Thanks for the column. My wife said you know more about my career than she does. You're a true Good Guy and I value our friendship." – WMCA "Good Guy" disc jockey Ed Baer.

"A lovely tribute to a lovely man." (In response to my article about the death of our mutual college professor.) – ABC News analyst George Stephanopoulos.

~

Attend two open mic readings. Watch and listen to the readers at the first one. Read a poem or story of your own at the second one. If there are no readings for you to attend, give a piece of your writing to three other people. Ask them to read it and to pass it along.

Scenes From an Ordinary Life

The earliest memory that I can affix a date to is from when I was just shy of three and a half years old. It was in November 1963, the day President Kennedy was assassinated. I was with my grandmother in the Bronx, New York. I can clearly picture the places we walked and the events that unfolded when we returned to her apartment on the Grand Concourse. More than thirty years later, those memories became the poem "Dateline Dallas" in my collection of memoir poems, *Permanent Records*. How accurate are my memories of that day and how much have they been molded by decades of looking back at them both with my grandmother over the years and after her death? That is not something I can answer, but that is the beauty of memoir.

It is the little moments that make up a lifetime – the euphoria, the downtrodden, the oppressive, and the uplifting – the nostalgic, the frightening, the joyous, the tragic, the unknown, and the routine – the sensual, and the embarrassing, the triumphant, and the forgotten. They are all of equal value when evaluating a life. A memoir is part diary, part photo album. Part scrapbook and part hope chest. It is a permanent record, subject to change, of that which while often too trivial to stay in the forefront of our lives for more than a moment, is too precious to ever lose.

Everyone has stories burning to be told. Memoir writing provides an opportunity to create a permanent record of the events that shaped our lives and a way to examine those events. These stories eliminate the common problem of having "nothing to write about." Memoirs help us find meaning in our lives. They allow meaningful moments to be revisited, and they often provide the opportunity to grapple with unresolved issues. They allow for meaningful connections to be made among times, places, people, and generations. They can be entertaining and instructive, stimulating and therapeutic. Memoirs help us gain insight and confidence while developing a clearer sense of self.

I have written and published many memoir pieces on topics including donating blood for the first time, visiting a replica of the Vietnam Veterans memorial, thumbing through a datebook from the year I graduated from high school and began college, and my son's little league team. None of these were about earth shattering events, yet met with enthusiastic response from my readers. These little memoir/diary based columns are not by any means a testament to my prowess as a writer, but rather validation that the little things are really the big ones after all.

"Old Datebook Rekindles Fond Memories of Twenty Years Ago"

It is the end of 1997 and most people are making plans for 1998. They will compile lists of things they would like to change about themselves and their lives. Goals and objectives will be recorded in newly purchased organizers.

The disappointments and joys of the year gone by will be recalled, all with the knowledge that with the flip of a calendar page, everything will start anew.

I have not been giving much thought to 1998. I have been basking in the memories of another year, one two decades old.

I recently came across a small plastic-covered datebook that I used in 1978. 1978 may not be a terribly significant year to many people. Sinatra never sang about it, but to me "It Was a Very Good Year."

It was the year I graduated from Carmel High School and began studies at Columbia University. It was a year of endings and beginnings and of good times and good people. Flipping through the pages, reading the notations jotted in the little boxes by a Putnam County kid with New York City visions is like opening a time capsule filled with friends and places and events suddenly as vivid now as they were then.

They are tinged, no doubt, with a slight hue of melancholy and at least a hint of longing, but if life has been good, there are not many regrets. The first entry carries over from the previous year.

December 31, 1977. It says, "New Year's Eve party," evoking images of welcoming 1978 with Jim Verderese, Bill Cassidy, Rob Krizek, and whomever we were dating at the time. It was the way we always started the new year, never imagining the miles the years would some day put between us.

Sprinkled throughout are notations of meetings, fundraisers, and trips-May 12-14 canoeing on the Westbend River in Vermont; climbing Mount Marcy June 16-19, all part of the local Explorer post directed by then Carmel, now Chappaqua school administrator Mark Soss. The names and faces of people met on those trips that were once forgotten, now come flooding back.

High school job hours appear at various times. January and February working on the remodeling crew at Barkers (later to become Kings, then Ames) in Putnam Plaza. June through August loading cars and trucks at Lloyd Lumber in Carmel which would be sold and ultimately reborn under the direction of my old boss, Carl Dill.

Naturally social "obligations" occupied much of my time, as with any high school senior. February 10 – senior prom (theme song "Beginnings" by Chicago.) March 1 – honor society trip to "The King and I" (starring Yul Brynner.) April 13 – Yankee game (it was a Thursday, so we ditched school.) April 23-28 – class trip to Disney World. Visits with Sue Truran, Brian Hill, and doing yard work for Herb Moore. June 13 – yearbook dedication dinner, with English teacher Jack Clarke as our honoree.

Parties and movies (*Saturday Night Fever* three times over two weekends) followed by hours of cruising to Billy Joel's *The Stranger* and Meatloaf's *Bat Out of Hell* then parking along back roads. 2 a.m. cheeseburgers at the Windmill Diner were regular occurrences along with bowling nights at Brewster Lanes.

On July 29, the datebook reads "Yankee Old Timers Day." My father and I in the stands the day Billy Martin, having been fired during the season, returned to the stadium with the announcement that he would return to manage the team again. Who knew then that it would become something of a stadium ritual?

The summer of 1978, while filled with friends and fun, also brings back a somber memory. In the box marked Monday, July 24, the notation says "Roland's Mass, 10 a.m.," a reference to our class president Roland Bartlett who died in an auto accident that summer.

I scan the pages again and find more reminders of the changes that two decades bring...birthdays of grandparents now gone; visiting a favorite aunt and uncle (also gone) in New Rochelle after attending a reception for incoming Columbia freshmen at a professor's nearby home on April 9. Seeing one of my heroes, Harry Chapin perform in a Central Park concert August 23. He would perish three years later.

By September, high school seemed a distant memory and college and life in the city was in full swing. Orientation week activities, guest lecturers like Jacques Cousteau on September 24; a Yankee playoff game on October 6, capping the wonderful season they spent chasing the Red Sox; meeting Jim who was in town for a college break at Grand Central to attend the auto show on November 19; meeting Rob for the Rockefeller Center tree lighting on December 4 and losing each other in the crowd.

Election Day that year was November 7, and I was assigned to cover the gubernatorial race for WKCR, the college radio station. After meeting Bella Abzug, John Tesh and Pia Lindstrom and taking care of the college station, I phoned in a report to Eric Gross, the news director at WPUT back home and had my first paid night as a journalist, earning ten dollars as a stringer.

Final exams that first semester were the week of December 18. The final notation in the book: December 31, 1978, "New Year's Eve party with Jim, Bill, and Rob."

So 1978 now recedes back to memory and 1998 begins with high school seniors entering prom dates and job hours and college orientations in their calendars to be waited for in anticipation, enjoyed, and then slowly, but inevitably, forgotten. Unless, of course, they safely tuck those datebooks away to be uncovered by a distant version of themselves…twenty years older, filled with experience, wisdom, and wistfulness, eager to return to that special year just one more time.

"It's About Baseball"

It is not about bomb threats in public schools, or air attacks on far off lands, or the latest trends on Wall Street. It is about everything that is good. It is about clichés that never sound like clichés – the greenest grass, the bluest skies, and everything that is good and pure and American.

It is about a cultural landscape where summer resorts in the Catskill Mountains, drive-in movie theaters, and diners with homemade pies are vanishing like automats, photo booths, and telephones with dials. It is about generations and of how one event summons another and of how sometimes the simplest things are the best things.

It is about baseball, and when all is said and done it will still be about baseball.

It is the first summer when a nation cannot turn its lonely eyes to the great DiMaggio. The perfectly tailored suit had long replaced the pinstripes, but it seemed that number five would always and forever be part of summer. It is about a summer when my boyhood favorite, Jim "Catfish" Hunter appeared at spring training, still the embodiment of class, his body betraying him as A.L.S. steals what is left of the fastball that once fashioned five consecutive 20 victory seasons.

It is about my son, Justin, number three on his back, playing his first season in the Kent Recreation Hot Shot League, a wonderful league for five and six year olds. A field of dreams behind the Kent Primary and Elementary Schools, where every batter hits one thousand and every team is a winner. He played, sometimes, against his friend Robbie Krizek's team-two young boys carrying on their fathers' passion for the sport.

Before we ever dreamed of having our own sons to play catch with, Robbie's dad Rob and I would take the Metro-North to the city and then the number seven subway to his grandmother's home in Jackson Heights or the D train to the

Bronx to catch a game at one of New York's stadiums. We were there to see Yankee skipper Joe Torre manage the Mets and we were there when candy bars named for Reggie Jackson showered the field in the Bronx after one of his mammoth home runs. We were there when Tom Seaver returned to Shea to hit two doubles and beat his former teammates for the Reds. Now, twenty years after a plane crash took Thurman Munson, our sons play baseball together and that is how it should be. A new generation making new baseball memories.

Justin watches Tino Martinez now and Derek Jeter and Bernie Williams too. He imitates the homerun calls of John Sterling and Michael Kay and knows instinctively that there is something special about baseball. I know that there will come a day when just a hint of those announcers' voices will bring back a flood of memories for him just as the voices of Phil Rizzuto, Bill White, and Frank Messer do for me.

Sure, the Yankees won a record 125 games last season, but did anyone bat a thousand? Did every batter cross home plate every inning? Did every player high five each opponent after each game? Kent Recreation has it right. Justin's "Purple Team" coach Don Meyer and Recreation Director Bill Huestes have it right too.

It is about generations and seasons and little boys who tap their bats on home plate and who, for a little while at least, know that every hit is a home run and every sky is blue and all the grass is green, and every team is a winner.

"Vietnam Veterans Memorial Touches Visitors in Many Ways"

In the final moments of Norman Jewison's film version of the Bobbie Ann Mason novel *In Country*, seventeen-year-old Samantha Hughes (Emily Lloyd) reaches out to the Vietnam Veterans Memorial and touches the name of the father she never knew – the father who died in the conflict before she was born.

Meanwhile, her uncle (Bruce Willis) a veteran who never fully adjusted to life after his time "in country" makes peace with his troubled past at the foot of the dark granite monument.

The healing they experienced is symbolic of a nation coming to terms with a haunting time in its recent past.

After at least a dozen viewings, the scene has still not lost its impact for me even though much about the time period was foreign to me. Perhaps any of us under the draft age during the American experience in Vietnam know that we should have strong feelings about the time period, but we have a difficult time sorting them out since Vietnam to us is as much a part of our pop culture as it is a part of our national heritage. I was too young to be drafted during the Vietnam era, just as my father was too young for World War II, and his father before him too young for World War I. Sometimes fate, it seems, can be genetic.

The campus protests were at most a faint memory during my years at Columbia University. The heartfelt songs of social consciousness ("Be the first one on your block to have your boy sent home in a box") now appear on golden oldies compilations. Still, as I viewed The Moving Wall, the half size replica of the Veterans Memorial at Putnam County Park near my home when it was on display, I began to understand why *In Country* has been such a haunting image to me, both as a book and a movie.

We are all simultaneously touched and troubled in some way by the American experience in Vietnam. Some of us are fortunate. We did not lose anyone close to us during the conflict. Some of us are lucky. We were not old enough to have been faced with the moral decisions that the draftees faced. We did not have to face the degradation of returning home from serving one's country in a foreign land and of being shunned by a public like no veterans had been before.

We all, however, live with and work with veterans or their children or someone with a more direct connection to the time than ourselves if we are among the lucky.

As I scanned the 58,196 names of the Americans who lost their lives during the Vietnam War, including the dozen from Putnam County, I looked at the same time into the eyes of my two-year-old son observing the wall and the torch in wide eyed amazement, not knowing of course the significance of it all, but somehow being taken in all the same. I listened as children, some too young to recall the Gulf War let alone Vietnam, read the names, one by one, over the public address system and 58,196 killed in Vietnam became the equivalent of 12 million killed in the Holocaust. There are ghosts to be felt. Stories to be recounted, slowly, one by one, after some time for healing has passed.

~

Write about the simple pleasures that you enjoy in your life.

The Thirty Books I Would Take to a Desert Island

The first thing I would do every year when moving back to campus and into my dorm room for the new school year was to organize my bookshelves. To this day, I do the same thing when setting up my classroom each September. I feel much more comfortable with books around. Any time I have a vacation approaching, I carefully select a book to be part of the experience. Books provide inspiration in style, tone, sometimes in just providing a level to which to aspire. Some books, even though I love them, can make me sad with the feeling that I may never write anything as good. Here in no particular order are thirty books that I would never want to be without. Ask me tomorrow or the next day, the list might change, but always there will be books that I never want to wander too far away from.

1. *Writing Down the Bones* – Natalie Goldberg
2. *The Art of Love* – Kenneth Koch
3. *The Godfather* – Mario Puzo
4. *The Summer of '98* – Mike Lupica
5. *A Drinking Life* – Pete Hamill
6. *In Country* – Bobbie Ann Mason
7. *A Walk to Remember* – Nicholas Sparks
8. *A Farewell to Arms* – Ernest Hemingway
9. *The Prince of Tides* – Pat Conroy
10. *The Old Neighborhood* – Avery Corman
11. *Be True to Your School* – Bob Greene
12. *The Bridges of Madison County* – Robert James Waller
13. *Ghost Light* – Frank Rich
14. *American Beat* – Bob Greene
15. *Forever* – Pete Hamill
16. *Cape Cod* – William Martin
17. *The Girl in the Picture* – Denise Chong
18. *Great Expectations* – Charles Dickens

19. *Rockin' America* – Rick Sklar
20. *The Girl Who Loved Tom Gordon* – Stephen King
21. *The Two of Us* – Peter Smith
22. *The Sweeps* – Mark Christensen and Cameron Smith
23. *Autobiography of a Face* – Lucy Grealy
24. *Tuesdays with Morrie* – Mitch Albom
25. *All the President's Men* – Carl Bernstein and Bob Woodward
26. *Wild Season* – Allen W. Eckert
27. *Good Enough to Dream* – Roger Kahn
28. *An Hour Before Daylight* – Jimmy Carter
29. *The Lovely Bones* – Alice Sebold
30. *In the Cherry Tree* – Dan Pope

Maybe I should expand the list a bit to include any or all of Robert B. Parker's Spenser novels and a couple of collections of Anna Quindlen's columns. Then there are the great plays like Thornton Wilder's *Our Town*, Lorraine Hansberry's *A Raisin in the Sun*, Tennessee Williams' *The Glass Menagerie*, and everything by Neil Simon. My list could hardly be complete without some poetry by Richard Brautigan, Lawrence Ferlinghetti, Jane Shore, and Frank O'Hara. Then there is *The Last Avant-Garde*, David Lehman's exceptional history of the New York School of Poets. I also need to include *The Five Little Peppers and How They Grew* by Margaret Sidney, which my maternal grandmother used to read to me. Elizabeth Berg's "Katie" trilogy (*Durable Goods*, *Joy School*, and *True to Form*) should be close at hand. I just finished Steve Martin's *The Pleasure of My Company* and must find a place for it on the list. And so it goes. You can never have enough books.

~

Make a list of books you love and think about how and why they have affected you.

Preventative Maintenance

Those of us old enough to remember the mimeograph machines used before Xerox came along remember sniffing the purple surface as the smell of alcohol filled our noses. Day after day those sheets formed the curriculum through which we were taught how to write. Traditionally, we were taught how to make the twenty-six letters of the alphabet. We grew up with Dick and Jane expanding our cache of words. We studied spelling lists and completed worksheet after worksheet of grammar and usage exercises. All of this was useful, but overall, formed the basic misunderstand about good writing. Grammar, usage, sentence and paragraph structure, all have a place, but are not the building blocks of good writing. They do not lay a foundation on which to build, but rather they serve as the final coat of paint on the trim of the finished house. It does not make it stronger fundamentally, but makes it look pretty and overall, a finished product. The true building block is a body of writing put down on paper.

I spent many years knowing that this was right. None of us became better writers by studying and being quizzed on grammar. Teachers always assumed that by learning to make the letters, combining them into words, and passing quizzes on the rules of mechanics, we could write. That would be like reading the rules of baseball and being able to hit the curveball. It takes practice and more practice.

I admit that as a teacher, my stance on grammar and usage has not always been a popular one. It is much easier to find consensus among fellow writers. There is a feeling of reluctance on the part of those not intimate with the writing process to abandon the traditional route. Filling pages with practice writing of any type and using good examples of published writing as models gives the budding and the veteran writer something to revise and polish. Rules of grammar, usage, and structure can be incorporated into one's repertoire of writing "tools" much more effectively within the context of actual pieces of writing, not isolated on worksheets and quizzes.

I understand the reluctance. Mechanics can be graded on a right or wrong basis, pieces of writing cannot.

I found some validation, at least on a personal level, at a Barnes & Noble bookstore in Danbury, Connecticut. I stopped in one day and by chance novelist S.E. Hinton (*The Outsiders, Tex, That was Then, This is Now*) was doing a talk and book signing. Someone in the crowd asked her about the need to know about grammar to write well. Her answer was that she felt that by writing and reading good writing, you pick up the rules and learn to use them. I told her that I had always found tremendous similarities between *The Outsiders* and the film *Rebel Without a Cause* and wondered if she had been influenced by the movie. She answered that she never thought about it, but that perhaps it was possible on a subconscious level. That too was validating. I believe that using good writing as models helps us develop our own styles while in a subtle way, preserving the styles of those who came before us.

When I was compiling my first poetry chapbook, *The Last Automat*, I looked back at some of my earlier poems and wondered how I could have ever thought of them as "polished" pieces and did not give a thought to including them in the book. Similarly, a few years later, when I was selecting poems from my chapbooks to include in my first full-length collection, *Composite Sketches*, I found some entries in the earlier books that were easy to exclude from the new book. I suspect that this will continue to be the pattern over the years. This is not meant to invalidate the earlier work. There is great value in looking back and seeing improvement and changes in your own style. Our early work is just that, early work that allows us to become better.

There is no magic formula for becoming a better writer, although almost all students and aspiring writers tend to grasp for something concrete to use as a set of guidelines. When I give an open ended writing prompt in a workshop, immediately hands go up around the room wanting to know "can I do this" or "am I allowed to do that." They want the security of something being either right or wrong. That cannot be a guiding force in writing. Still, it makes people more comfortable, so here in no particular order, are some suggestions that might serve as "preventative maintenance" for writers; a few things you can keep in mind while still writing with the sense of uncontrolled recklessness that should guide your writing.

1. *Nobody is a born writer.* You get better at it by doing it. Michael Jordan was not born with a basketball under his arm.

2. *Everyone can learn to write well.* You don't need to be Hemingway or Fitzgerald to have something to say that others might like to hear. You do not always recognize that you are honing your craft. As kids we would write little parodies of television shows and act them out in my backyard. Back then, I never dreamed that there was a connection between that type of writing and the writing we did in school.

3. *You need not look for something "important" to write about.* Anything important or interesting to you is good enough.

4. *Writing should involve taking risks.* Don't most things you find exhilarating involve some sort of danger, or at least a possibility of failure?

5. *There is no such thing as writer's block.* Write something terrible and then revise it. In baseball, players might go into slumps, but they work through them. They don't call them "blocks" and hang up their spikes.

6. *Bad writing is valuable.* It gives you something to work with, and it often leads to good writing; it can always serve as a bad example.

7. *While it is all right to use one, do not be limited by an outline.* Let one thing lead to another. My poem "Composite Sketches" not only led to my chapbook

Summer Rising, River Flowing, but also to a new way of looking at my own poetic process. I began to see my poems as composites of past, present, future, reality, and fantasy all joined together.

8. *Find a grammar and usage handbook that you are comfortable with and think of it as a medicine chest.* You don't open the door above the bathroom sink and use every item you find behind it in a row-by-row orderly fashion. You take what you need for what ails you. Dealing with grammar and usage should be the same. Studying a textbook cover to cover does not make you a better writer. Read good writing and be able to use a writing handbook the same as you would a dictionary, to look up what you happen to need at a given moment.

9. *Be brave enough to edit.* Overwriting is a good idea, then go back and keep the parts that work the best. Beware of first sentences in paragraphs, first lines in poems, and first paragraphs in longer pieces of writing. They can almost always be removed thus improving the writing. This is because there is a natural tendency to explain or introduce what we will be writing about instead of getting straight to the point. What you leave out can be as important as what you leave in.

10. *Apply the basic writing process for formal writing tasks.* Think about what you know about your topic. Many books call this brainstorming or pre-writing. Organize your thoughts and ideas. This is often referred to as outlining, although I consider the term too limiting. Produce a first draft without worrying about how good it is, just go from start to finish. Do some revising, without ever using the term "final draft." Eventually you will be finished, but it is better to never consider a piece of writing to be final.

11. *Interact with other writers.* It is always useful to get some feedback from someone else who is intimate with the writing process, but not necessarily with you. The more someone loves you, the less comfortable he or she might be being honest with you about the areas that need improvement.

12. *Make writing a priority and write regularly.* If you do not consider it an important activity in your life and let others know that it is important, you will never get where you want to be as a writer.

13. *Be specific and use details.* If you were being set up on a blind date would you prefer that the person be described to you simply as "he" or "she" or would you like some information that painted more of a picture in your mind?

14. *Make a one-to-one connection with each of your readers.* In radio the first piece of advice is to talk on the air as if to one person. Each person in your audience can feel that he or she is being addressed directly, that the broadcast is uniquely his or hers. Writing should be approached in the same way.

15. *Get a reaction – good or bad.* The television commercials that are effective in selling products are the ones we really love and the ones we really hate. They are equally good at influencing our buying habits because we remember them. Make your readers remember you.

16. *Read like a writer.* Think about how whatever you are reading has been structured. What has the writer tried to do with words and how? The more you write, the more you will read with a writer's eye.

17. *Market yourself and your work.* Nobody else will do it for you.

18. *Don't give up*. After many attempts, my first national publication was a one-line excerpt from an article I had submitted to *English Journal*. It was enough to motivate me to keep trying and eventually I landed articles there and many other places.

19. *Have fun*. Writing can be frustrating and sometimes tedious work, but the satisfaction when something comes together and the words do what you want them to is unequalled.

~

Take a piece you have written, correct for grammar and usage. Make each sentence flow as smoothly as you can, then rewrite the piece using only half as many words as you started with.

About the Author

Lou Orfanella is a New York based teacher and writer. He holds degrees from Columbia University and Fordham University. He is the author of the poetry collections *Composite Sketches*, *Permanent Records*, *Summer Rising*, *River Flowing*, and *The Last Automat*. He contributed a chapter to the book *Rationales for Teaching Young Adult Literature* and has published over one hundred articles, essays, columns, reviews, and poems in numerous national and regional magazines, newspapers, and journals. He does frequent public readings of his work and teaches writing at Western Connecticut State University and English in the Valhalla, New York school district. He offers individual instruction and group workshops on topics including poetry, memoir, journalism, fiction, and family history. He can be contacted by e-mail at LORFANELLA@hotmail.com.

Also available from Fine Tooth Press:

Fiction
Pressure Points by Craig Wolf
Hardboiled Egg by Oscar De Los Santos
The Massabesic Murders by Gypsey Teague
To Beat a Dead Horse by Bill Campbell
Trickster Tales by JP Briggs
White River by Will Bless
Trespass by Craig Wolf

Non-Fiction
Spirits of Texas and New England by Oscar De Los Santos
Breakout by L.R. Wright

Poetry
Composite Sketches by Lou Orfanella
Balloons Over Stockholm by James R. Scrimgeour

In the Works:
A Poet's Guide to Divorce by David Breedan
Desperate Straits by Esther Schrader
Reel Rebels edited by Oscar De Los Santos
Street Angel by Martha Marinara
Border Cantos by Chuck Etheridge
Typical Girl by Donna Kuhn
Darkscapes by Steven Wedel
Looking for a Face Like Mine: The History of African-Americans in Comics by William H. Foster III
New Goddess: Transgendered Women in the Twenty-First Century edited by Gypsey Teague

For more information about these and other titles, as well as author bios and interviews and more, visit us on the web at:

http://www.finetoothpress.com